anythink

D0578650

The New South and the Old West

1866–1890

DISCOVERING U.S. HISTORY

The New World: Prehistory–1542

Colonial America: 1543–1763

Revolutionary America: 1764–1789

Early National America: 1790–1850

The Civil War Era: 1851–1865

The New South and the Old West: 1866–1890

The Gilded Age and Progressivism: 1891–1913

World War I and the Roaring Twenties: 1914–1928

The Great Depression: 1929–1938

World War II: 1939–1945

The Cold War and Postwar America: 1946–1963

Modern America: 1964–Present

DISCOVERING U.S. HISTORY

The New South and the Old West
1866–1890

Tim McNeese

Consulting Editor: Richard Jensen, Ph.D.

CHELSEA HOUSE
PUBLISHERS
An imprint of Infobase Publishing

THE NEW SOUTH AND THE OLD WEST: 1866–1890

Chelsea House
An imprint of Infobase Publishing
132 West 31st Street
New York NY 10001

Library of Congress Cataloging-in-Publication Data
McNeese, Tim.
  The New South and the Old West, 1866–1890 / by Tim McNeese.
      p. cm. — (Discovering U.S. history)
  Includes bibliographical references and index.
  ISBN 978-1-60413-354-7 (hardcover)
  1. Reconstruction (U.S. history, 1865–1877)—Juvenile literature. 2. United States—History—1865–1898—
Juvenile literature. 3. West (U.S.)—History—1860–1890—Juvenile literature. 4. Frontier and pioneer life—
West (U.S.)—Juvenile literature. 5. Cowboys—West (U.S.)—19th century—History—Juvenile literature.
6. Indians of North America—Wars—West (U.S.)—Juvenile literature. 7. Indians of North America—
Wars—1866–1895—Juvenile literature. I. Title. II. Series.

E668.M157 2009
978'.02—dc22

                              2009006647

The Discovering U.S. History series was produced for Chelsea House by
Bender Richardson White, Uxbridge, UK

Editors: Lionel Bender and Susan Malyan
Designer and Picture Researcher: Ben White
Production: Kim Richardson
Maps and graphics: Stefan Chabluk
Cover printed by Bang Printing, Brainerd, MN
Book printed and bound by Bang Printing, Brainerd, MN
Date printed: April 2010
Printed in the United States of America

10 9 8 7 6 5 4 3 2 1

Contents

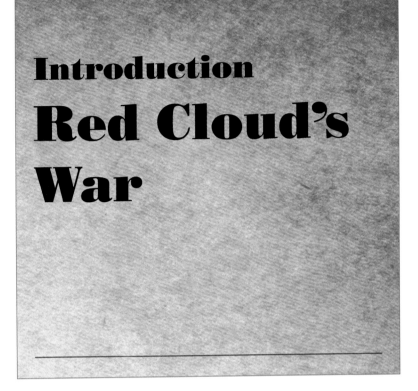

Introduction
Red Cloud's War

Indian tepees stretched for a mile (1.6 kilometers) or more away from Fort Laramie, a western army post nestled between the Laramie and Platte Rivers in the Nebraska Territory (today's Wyoming). The date was June 1866. Native American leaders representing powerful nations from the northern Great Plains—the Cheyenne, Arapaho, and bands of the Teton Sioux, including the Brule, Miniconjou, and Oglala—had gathered once again, at the request of the U.S. government, to talk about the future of the American West.

A WARRIOR NAMED RED CLOUD
One of the chiefs present was an Oglala, named Makhpiya-Luta. The white men at the fort knew him as Red Cloud. This 44-year-old warrior was legendary. He had accumulated 80 coups, or military victories, in his long career. During the previous three years he had led younger warriors in a campaign against the encroachment of whites onto Indian

lands. During the early 1860s, with a gold rush underway in today's Montana, whites were crawling all over Sioux lands. In 1862 a prospector named John M. Bozeman had carved out a trail from Fort Laramie to Bannack, Montana, to facilitate the movement of Americans into the gold camps around Bannack. This road crossed Indian land that had been ceded to the Sioux under the 1851 Fort Laramie Treaty. It cut across the Powder River country, one of the last regions of the West where the great bison herds still roamed undisturbed by the advance of Anglo-American civilization. Red Cloud and his followers were not prepared to allow such an immigrant road through their western domain.

In 1863 Bozeman himself, along with a wagon train of mining supplies, had been turned back by Sioux warriors, led by Chief Red Cloud. By 1865 U.S. Army troops were patrolling the Bozeman Trail. Chief Red Cloud and his warriors had defied the army and fought to keep the mining road closed. Although Red Cloud belonged to the Oglala band of the Teton Sioux, he and his followers were aided by other Teton bands, including the Brules, Hunkpapas, Miniconjous, and Sans Arcs. The Sioux had fought hard and relentlessly against the army into the summer of 1866.

Talks at Fort Laramie

Now the government had called Red Cloud and other Indian leaders to Fort Laramie to negotiate. At first the talks between white government agents and the Indian leaders seemed promising. Federal officials were ready to offer Red Cloud and the others an annual payment of $75,000, accompanied by a promise to never wrest the Powder River Country away from them.

Then, with the talks still underway, a lengthy column of infantrymen, followed by a fleet of army wagons, arrived at the fort, led by Colonel Henry Beebe Carrington, who was carrying orders. Curious, one of the negotiating chiefs asked the newly arrived officer where he was headed. Carrington then revealed his orders: He was to march to the Bozeman Trail, where his men were to build two additional forts to protect the white trail to the mining camps.

Suddenly Red Cloud erupted in anger. His words were immediate and final, as noted by historian Jon Lewis:

> *The Great Father sends us presents and wants us to sell him the road, but White Chief goes with soldiers to steal the road before Indians say Yes or No! I will talk with you no more! I will go now, and I will fight you! As long as I live I will fight you for the last hunting grounds of my people.*

Defiant as ever, Red Cloud left the negotiations and the fort with his warriors. Once again the Powder River Country would run red with blood.

TROUBLE ALONG THE POWDER RIVER

Colonel Carrington and his men marched out of Fort Laramie on June 21 and, within a week, reached Fort Reno on the Bozeman Trail. Indians wasted no time in harassing Carrington, driving off almost all of the fort's horses the following day. Moving on, Carrington reached the fork of the Powder and the Little Piney rivers and construction on Fort Phil Kearny began.

Red Cloud remained true to his promise to fight the army, usually through regular hit-and-run raids. His warriors engaged in no direct frontal attacks, relying on ambushes and quick raids that caused a steady drain on Carrington's manpower and other resources. Within weeks of the failure of the talks at Fort Laramie, U.S. troops at Fort Kearny were experiencing a killing, wounding, or scalping of a soldier each day. A reporter-photographer from a popular Eastern publication, *Frank Leslie's Illustrated Newspaper,* ventured too far from the fort and was found naked, his body split open by a tomahawk.

A worried Colonel Carrington sent letters to his superiors, pleading for more men. A man of little experience, Carrington was a lawyer in civilian life, and had spent much of the Civil War as a desk-bound administrator. Most of his requests were denied, but a handful of soldiers were sent to Fort Phil Kearny, including a dashing young captain, a veteran of the Civil War, named William Judd Fetterman. As Carrington dithered over his "Indian problem," Fetterman was too quick to disregard the threat Red Cloud and his men represented. Soon after his arrival at the fort along the Powder River, Fetterman bragged, notes historian Jon Lewis: "Give me a single company of regulars and I can whip a thousand Indians. With eighty men I could ride through the Sioux nation."

A DOOMED PARTY

He would not have to wait long to prove his claim. In December a party of soldiers was sent out of Fort Phil Kearny to cut and gather firewood, and soon came under attack. Hearing gunfire, a rescue party was dispatched from the fort, under the command of Captain William Fetterman. Carrington had first selected another officer to lead the rescue, but Fetterman had insisted he be given the duty, as he technically outranked Carrington's first choice. Carrington agreed, against his better judgment, but gave orders to the brash captain not to pursue the Indians past Lodge Trail Ridge.

When Fetterman and his men reached the wood party, the Indians scattered. Fetterman was confident he had driven them away, but minutes later a small party of warriors on horseback sped into view, led by a Lakota destined for fame, Crazy Horse.

A Sioux Encampment— an oil painting from about 1880 by Jules Tavernier. The Native Americans moved their encampments across the Plains as they followed the herds of buffalo—their main source of food, clothing material, and cooking utensils.

Somewhat slightly built, Crazy Horse was not impressive at first sight, a fighter who was not prone to bragging. But he was a fearless opponent of the U.S. Army. As another Oglala war leader, He Dog, later said of Crazy Horse, notes historian Robert Utley: "Crazy Horse always led his men himself when they went into battle and he kept well in front of them. He headed many charges." For Fetterman, Crazy Horse represented one more Indian warrior that he simply underestimated.

Crazy Horse and his men, all followers of Red Cloud, rushed toward Fetterman's soldiers, waving blankets and taunting them. The troopers opened fire, but Crazy Horse dismounted, putting himself within range of his enemy's rifles, seemingly unafraid. Then the Indians began to fall back, heading up the slope toward Lodge Trail Ridge. A confident Fetterman, certain that he had his Indian antagonists on the run, ordered his men forward.

But the army captain's confidence soon faded. While pursuing Crazy Horse and fewer than a dozen Indians, Fetterman fell into a trap, as he and his men were surrounded by hundreds of Arapaho, Northern Cheyenne, and Sioux warriors. Suddenly a dozen Indian warriors had mushroomed into a dizzying 2,000 fierce fighters. The fight only took a matter of minutes. The soldiers, taking defensive positions behind dead ponies, fought bravely, but they were overwhelmed. They simply ran out of ammunition. As for Fetterman, he and a captain chose suicide over surrender, aiming their army-issue revolvers at each other's heads and pulling the triggers. Before it was over, Fetterman and 80 soldiers were killed. The Fetterman Massacre was the worst in U.S. Army history at the hands of Indians in more than a century.

Red Cloud had promised to fight for the lands that he felt belonged to his people. He had already fought the army, miners, and civilians along the Powder River and the road he hated for three years. At every turn, his tactics had paid off. He had harassed and mystified all opponents. He was supported by thousands of western warriors, men ready to fight and die for the only piece of ground they believed they had left. For decades Red Cloud had watched as countless thousands of Anglo-Americans had encroached onto Lakota lands. He had watched as the great bison herds of his boyhood shrank to smaller and smaller circles of animals. He had now determined to fight or die. By the end of 1866, after three successful years on the path of war, Red Cloud appeared to be winning.

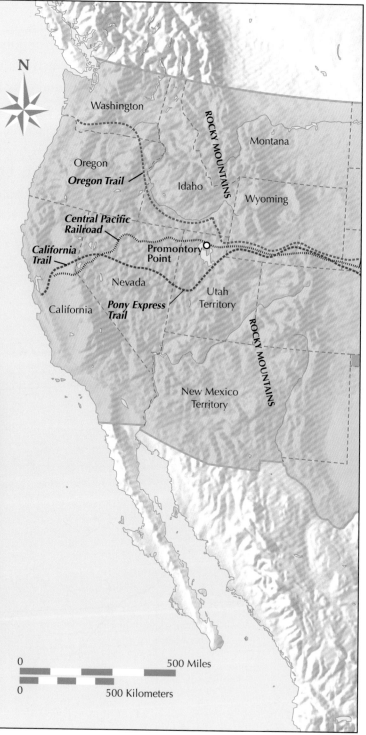

By 1890 the United States comprised 44 states that stretched from the Atlantic to the Pacific coast and from Canada to Mexico. Five railroads stretched from east to west, and cattle trails ran from Texas north across the Great Plains. Overland trails led from the Mississippi to California, Washington, and Oregon.

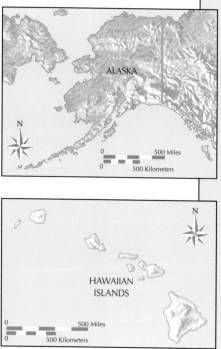

14

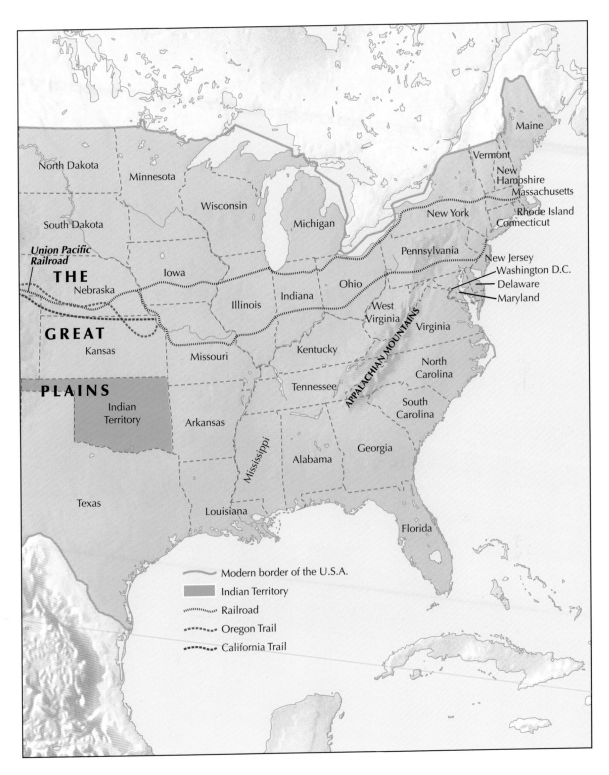

North Dakota

Minnesota

Maine

Vermont

New
Hampshire

Massachusetts

Wisconsin

Michigan

New York

Rhode Island
Connecticut

South Dakota

*Union Pacific
Railroad*

THE

Pennsylvania

New Jersey

Washington D.C.

Delaware

Maryland

Iowa

Ohio

Nebraska

Illinois

Indiana

West
Virginia

GREAT

Virginia

Kansas

Missouri

Kentucky

APPALACHIAN MOUNTAINS

North
Carolina

PLAINS

Tennessee

Indian
Territory

South
Carolina

Arkansas

Mississippi

Alabama

Georgia

Texas

Louisiana

Florida

⌇⌇⌇ Modern border of the U.S.A.

▨ Indian Territory

⌇⌇⌇ Railroad

▪▪▪ Oregon Trail

▪▪▪ California Trail

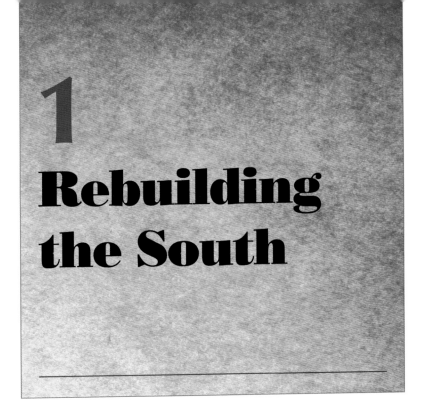

1

Rebuilding the South

In the spring of 1865 the national nightmare of the Civil War was over. Four years of bitter, violent conflict had torn the United States into two nations: one fighting to put political distance between itself and the old republic, and the other struggling to force its former Southern states to return to the national fold. But the issues that had divided the nation in 1861—state's rights, the expansion of slavery, even the continued existence of slavery—first had to be settled by war. Ultimately, the war had played itself out—the North had emerged triumphant, and the South was shattered. Yet, even as the cannon were silenced, the rifles stacked, and the sabers returned to their scabbards, binding the wounds caused by the war was not a simple process. Questions abounded. How should the country be restored? Should the South be further punished for the "treason" of secession? Who was to decide on a course of action—Congress, the President, the American people? How long should it take to restore the United States? What rights would be granted to former black slaves?

AT WAR'S END

By the end of the Civil War moderate Republican leaders in Congress saw their task of bringing the country back together as a matter of restoration. They wanted to see the Southern states become, once again, loyal to the United States government, with the reestablishment of each state's representation in Congress, including its representatives and senators. But more radical elements saw their opportunity to bring significant reconstruction to the South. They could take advantage of the moment and require the former states of the Confederacy to provide new opportunities for their newly freed black populations. As a leading House Republican, Thaddeus Stevens had his concerns, notes historian Robert Remini:

> *We have turned over, or are about to turn loose, four million slaves without a hut to shelter them or a cent in their pockets. The infernal laws of slavery have prevented them from an education, understanding of the commonest laws of contract, or of managing the ordinary business of life. This Congress is bound to provide for them until they can take care of themselves.*

For Southerners, many of whom had faced defeat and loss during the war, the hope was for redemption. They felt the war had destroyed their former world, their very ways of life. Many former Confederates believed the country could not be truly reunited until Southerners were allowed to take control of their states, their politics, and their futures.

For almost a dozen years between 1865 and 1877, a period three times longer than the Civil War itself, the country engaged in an era known as Reconstruction. During these years America's leaders struggled with all three goals—restoration, reconstruction, and redemption. They ultimately emerged with the nation intact, but still damaged, as some of its loftier goals, including recognizing the rights and freedoms of its black citizens, were lost in the conflict between Congress and the President.

LINCOLN'S RECONSTRUCTION

Even before the end of the Civil War, President Abraham Lincoln announced his plan for Reconstruction. In part it was a plan to convince Southerners to give up the secessionist cause and return to the Union. Lincoln announced his program in December 1863, and it was soon dubbed the "Ten Percent Plan." The President would grant pardons to all Confederates who swore a loyalty oath to support the U.S. Constitution and to accept the destruction of slavery. Only high Confederate officials and military officers would not be pardoned. When the number of people who took the oath in a given state was equal to 10 percent of the number of people who had voted there during the 1860 election, state officials could establish a new state government and apply to be readmitted into the Union. All new state constitutions submitted to Congress would have to include a prohibition of slavery. Otherwise, the reconstructed states would be free from additional restrictions by the federal government.

Lincoln's whole plan of Reconstruction was based on streamlining the way for states to be readmitted to the Union, while not making any attempt to further punish any Confederate state or its people. His was not a plan of retribution, but one of forgiveness. And, although the plan did not require the seceded states to include blacks in the process or provide any significant role for former slaves in remolding Southern politics, it did guarantee that slavery would

A photograph of freed slaves and a Union soldier in Beaufort, South Carolina. The slaves became known as Beaufort Contrabands since they had been illegally transported to within Union lines during the Civil War.

have no future in a restored Union. Lincoln did suggest that some blacks should be allowed to vote, especially those with enough education to make reasonable political decisions. No previous president had ever proposed black suffrage on a general basis.

But, even as Lincoln presented his plan for reconstructing the Union, some members of Congress were not certain that it was within his scope of power to determine that process. Under the U.S. Constitution, as laid out in Article IV, Section 3, it was the Congress that admitted states into the Union, not the president. However, the Constitution had been written to deal with the admission of new states. The Founding Fathers had not worded the Constitution to facilitate the readmission of seceded states back into the country. It did not take long before a serious debate was underway between President Lincoln and the Republican leaders in Congress over which branch of government—executive or legislative—would set the direction of Reconstruction.

THE WADE-DAVIS BILL

Complicating matters were issues concerning slavery and its ultimate demise. During the war House member Thaddeus Stevens of Pennsylvania and Senator Charles Sumner of Massachusetts led the radical faction of the Republican Party in support of ending slavery and guaranteeing the basic rights of the South's blacks after slavery was ended. One of their concerns was purely political, however. They knew that, if the South was reconstructed without blacks gaining the right to vote, Democrats would control Southern politics just as they had before the war. If blacks gained the vote, the Radical Republicans believed they would gain a base of support for their party among these new voters. This was important to the Radicals, because they thought the result might otherwise mean that a war had been fought, with hundreds of thousands of men dying, only to restore the Union back to exactly the way it was before the outbreak of hostilities in 1861, even if slavery was no more.

Therefore, the reconstruction plan put together by Republicans in Congress proved quite different from Lincoln's plan. Their plan was presented in 1864 as the Wade-Davis Bill, sponsored by Senator Benjamin Wade of Ohio and Maryland Congressman Henry Winter Davis. Rather than relying on just 10 percent of voters taking a loyalty oath, the Wade-Davis plan demanded loyalty oaths by a majority of white males in a state. Anyone who had supported the Confederacy would not be eligible to vote and, in addition to eliminating slavery, the Southern states were to write guarantees of black equality into their state constitutions.

When the Wade-Davis Bill reached President Lincoln's desk for his signature in the summer of 1864, he refused—a political tactic called a pocket veto. One complication for Lincoln was that two Confederate states, Louisiana and Arkansas, had already created new state governments under his plan, even if Congress had not approved their moves. Without the president's signature, the Wade-Davis Bill died. Yet Lincoln announced that he would enforce the bill if any of the other nine Confederate states wanted to adopt it. On August 5, Wade and Davis lashed out against Lincoln's pocket veto, publishing their manifesto in the *New York Tribune*, a stinging indictment of Lincoln: "Congress passed a bill; the President refused to approve it, and then by proclamation puts as much of it in force as he sees fit . . . A more studied outrage on the legislative authority of the people has never been perpetrated." The denouncement continued, suggesting to Lincoln that, "if he wishes our support, he must confine himself to his Executive duties—to obey and to execute, not to make the laws—to suppress by arms armed rebellion, and leave political reorganization to Congress."

LINCOLN AND NEW LEGISLATION

Lincoln read their words, took them as a warning, then continued to pursue his own goals for Reconstruction. He did cooperate with Congress by signing another bill, one that created the Bureau of Refugees, Freedmen, and Abandoned Lands, popularly referred to as the Freedmen's Bureau. The general purpose of the new legislation was to protect the legal rights of former slaves across the South through a government agency. The work of the Freedmen's Bureau also included creating schools for black children, providing medical care and giving freed blacks opportunities to acquire or lease free Southern land for farming.

The President also cooperated with Congress on the passage of the Thirteenth Amendment, which abolished the institution of slavery in the United States. Lincoln's earlier executive order, the Emancipation Proclamation, had only applied to slaves in Confederate states, not the slave-holding "border states"—those that allowed slavery but had not seceded from the Union. The bill, passed in January 1865, was signed by Lincoln and finally ratified by the states the following December.

THE DEATH OF LINCOLN

Lincoln's days of determining the direction of Reconstruction did not last much longer, however. His focus remained the same: to restore the Union without severely punishing the South. Even the words of his Second Inaugural Address, delivered on March 4, 1865, mirrored this sentiment:

> *With malice toward none, with charity for all, with firmness in the right... let us strive on to finish the work we are in, to bind up the nation's wounds... to do all which may achieve and cherish a just and lasting peace among ourselves and with all nations.*

But, in April 1865, just five days after the surrender of General Robert E. Lee to General Grant at Appomattox Courthouse, Virginia, a Southern sympathizer and local actor named John Wilkes Booth shot Lincoln at point-blank range while the President was attending a comedic play at a theater in Washington, D.C. Vice President Andrew Johnson was sworn in to the presidency just three hours after Lincoln's passing.

JOHNSON IN POWER

The new president was a simple man, a former tailor from Tennessee, who had not learned to read or write until adulthood, with his wife as his tutor. Johnson had grown up hating the Southern planter class, feeling they were always oppressing and looking down their noses at the underclass of white Southerners like him. Johnson wasted little time making things clear regarding his stance on Reconstruction. He was not Lincoln, and he did not intend to be lenient with the former Confederate states.

Johnson wanted to provide support for the South's blacks. Even back in 1864, while he was running for vice president, Johnson had promised blacks: "I will be your Moses, and lead you through the Red Sea of War and Bondage to the fairer future of Liberty and Peace." It appeared, at least initially, that President Johnson and Congress might see eye to eye regarding the direction and intent of Reconstruction. He had, after all, been the only senator from a Confederate state who had continued to support the Union in 1861. However, Johnson never really embraced either role, whether that of the punisher of Southern secession or the great defender of the freedmen.

Several important factors probably worked against Johnson and his ultimate cooperation with the Radical Republicans in Congress. To begin, he was not a Republican, but

LINCOLN'S ASSASSINATION

It is still remembered as one of the saddest days in American history—Good Friday, April 14, 1865. The Civil War had ended on Palm Sunday (April 9) with the surrender of Southern General Robert E. Lee to General Ulysses S. Grant at Appomattox. President Abraham Lincoln had led the North through four years of war and was ecstatic that the dual national nightmares of secession and war might soon be over. To celebrate, he took First Lady Mary Todd Lincoln to Ford's Theater, just a few blocks from the White House, to see a play. But that evening would end tragically for the president, his wife, and the nation.

Lincoln was shot by John Wilkes Booth, a popular stage actor, for whom Ford's Theater was a second home. Booth, a misled Southern sympathizer, was upset that the war had ended with Southern defeat. He and a small group of conspirators had been intent on killing Lincoln for several months. On April 14, as Booth stopped by around noon at Ford's Theater to pick up his mail, he was informed that Lincoln and Grant would be attending a play there together that very evening. Suddenly Booth sprang into action. He intended to kill the president himself, using a 44-caliber, single shot Pennsylvania Derringer, then stab Grant.

The Lincolns arrived at the theater late, along with their guests, an engaged couple, Major Henry Rathbone and Clara Harris, the daughter of a U.S. senator. The Grants had bowed out earlier in the day to make a trip out of Washington. The Lincolns were led to the presidential box, situated at left of and above the stage, where the president seated himself in a rocking chair. Completely familiar with the theater, Booth went upstairs and entered a narrow hallway between the balcony and Lincoln's box, locking the door behind him. Quietly, he entered the box and took his place behind the president, unseen. Knowing the play, he waited until actor Harry Hawk spoke a humorous line. Then, as the audience laughed loudly, Booth pulled the trigger and changed the course of history.

a Jacksonian Democrat from Tennessee, and one who had owned slaves himself. In addition, he did not support blacks as he promised. Even by 1867 he was expressing his belief that blacks did not have the capacity to govern themselves, due to their latent inferiority. Back in 1863, when a Union officer complained that President Lincoln had redirected the war by issuing his Emancipation Proclamation, Johnson shouted, as historian James McPherson notes: "Damn the Negroes! I am fighting these traitorous aristocrats, their masters!"

As for punishing the Confederate states, it never happened with Johnson. Within a month of becoming president, Johnson began issuing pardons to those who had engaged in rebellion against the United States, in exchange for personal loyalty oaths to the U.S. government. The only exceptions were high-ranking Rebel officers and public officials, and those who owned property worth more than $20,000, a considerable figure at that time. With that exclusion, Johnson was punishing those "traitorous aristocrats" he so despised. He appointed governors for the former Confederate states and ordered state conventions with only white men making decisions. He did expect these conventions to support the Thirteenth Amendment. As for former slaves, Johnson thought they should cooperate, continue to work for their former masters, and stay out of politics. Just as Lincoln had done, Johnson tried to control the direction of Reconstruction.

BLACK CODES

With no restraints placed on them by President Johnson's plan of Reconstruction, Southern white political leaders began passing Black Codes to further restrict the newly freed blacks in their states. These laws were intended to limit the freedoms and rights of Southern blacks. They barred blacks from voting, serving on juries and testifying in court. Blacks could not carry a gun, loiter on public property, consume alcohol, hunt, or fish. Sometimes former slaves who could prove they had new employment would have to sign a labor contract that forced them to work for a white employer, perhaps the very master who had owned them as a slave.

When Congress came into session in December 1865, they were met by President Johnson assuring them that Reconstruction was, for all practical purposes, already completed, with acceptable state governments established in all of the former Confederate states.

The Radicals Fight Back

Seeing little difference between those who had held political power in the South before the war and those who now held power in 1865, the Radical Republicans had no intentions of allowing Reconstruction to slip out of their fingers. In the early spring of 1866 Congress created two new bills to support blacks across the South. The first added to the tenure of the Freedmen's Bureau by continuing funding. The other was the Civil Rights Act of 1866. This law stated that all persons born in the United States (although Indians were not included) were American citizens, regardless of race or whether they had been slaves earlier. Thus, all had the same legal rights, with the exception of voting. It represented landmark legislation, notes historian Remini, as "the first statutory definition of the right of American citizenship."

Johnson immediately vetoed both bills, stating that he believed both to threaten the power of the states in controlling their own affairs. At the end of the Civil War, Congress was majority Republican by three to one and, since many Southern Congressmen had not been seated yet, Congress now easily overrode Johnson's objections. Then, with Radical Republicans fearful that an influx of Southern Democrats into the Congress might overturn the new Civil Rights Act, the Republican leadership sent the Fourteenth Amendment for the states to ratify. This amendment stated that all native-born or naturalized persons were to be considered citizens of the United States, as well as of their respective states. This was to apply even to former slaves. Thus, a state could not deny the equal protection of the law to any of its citizens. The amendment also denied former Confederate officeholders the right to hold any new state or national office.

JOHNSON LOSES SUPPORT

Johnson responded with anger and desperation against such bold steps on the part of the Radical Republicans. He visited Congress and gave a speech, but almost no one cared. As historian Hans Trefousse notes, the *New York Tribune* reported the event with no sympathy for the President: "Mr. Johnson rode his hobby [horse] into Congress yesterday. Nobody wanted him, nobody expected him, nobody felt he had any business there. His message was about as appropriate as though it had contained the bill of fare for his breakfast, his latest tailor's account, or his opinions upon the cause of thunder." In August the President set out on a nation-wide speaking tour, which some jokingly referred to as a "swing around the circle," decrying the Radical Republicans and supporting the South and its white leadership. Audience members jeered at him and heckled the President with insults. General Grant agreed to go on the tour with him, but became so embarrassed by Johnson's behavior that he dropped out, claiming he was ill.

Johnson had made such a fool of himself that he further lost political support. When the mid-term elections were held in November, new Republican majorities were voted in. In the meantime all but one of the eleven former Confederate states refused to ratify the Fourteenth Amendment.

An American cartoon of 1867 deriding Secretary of State William H. Seward for having made a bad deal over the purchase of Alaska from Russia. From the start of Johnson's presidency, Congress was under pressure from Seward to secure this territory for the nation. Most citizens considered the area a frozen waste. Eventually on April 9, 1867, the territory was purchased for $7.2 million.

Southerners opposed the amendment because it provided too many rights for blacks. Ironically, once the amendment was approved, it ended the old three-fifths clause of the U.S. Constitution. As a result, 12 new southern seats were added in Congress when all the former Confederate states were finally added back into the Union.

CLIPPING THE PRESIDENT'S WINGS

Congress then took new steps to redefine Reconstruction, passing the First Reconstruction Act in early March 1867. Against Johnson's wishes and over his veto, the South was divided into five military districts, each placed into the hands of a major general in the U.S. Army. Federal troops were sent to each district to enforce the new legislation passed by Congress, which required the army to register all black men to vote. At least part of the motivation for the militarizing of the South was due to violent conditions across the former Confederate states during the spring and summer of 1866. Riots broke out in Memphis and New Orleans. In Memphis fights began between the black and white drivers of horse-drawn hacks, or cabs, across the city, ending in nearly 50 deaths and several rapes of black women. Schools, churches, and other public buildings were burned. In New Orleans several blacks were killed in the very hall where the state's constitutional convention had taken up its efforts for readmission to the Union.

Congressional leaders then established a new set of rules by which Southern state governments could be organized. First, the states had to call a constitutional convention with blacks among the delegates. Former Confederate leaders were still barred from participation. Any new state constitution had to include voting rights for blacks and the new legislatures had to vote in favor of the Fourteenth Amendment. Only then, could any former Rebel state rejoin the Union.

To keep Johnson's role in directing Reconstruction to a minimum, Congress passed the Tenure of Office Act. The act was aimed squarely at the president, denying him the power to remove officeholders, including his own cabinet members, without the approval of the Senate. In passing the act, Representative Thaddeus Stevens said, notes historian Remini, "Though the President is Commander-in-Chief, Congress is his commander; and God wiling, he shall obey. He and his minions shall learn that this is not a Government of kings. . . but a Government of the people, and that Congress is the people." The stage was set for an epic duel between the executive and legislative branches.

Again, President Johnson responded with indignation and, perhaps, rightly so. He considered the Tenure Act to be unconstitutional. To test the legislation, he ordered the dismissal of Secretary of War Edwin M. Stanton, who had supported the Radical Republicans. House Republicans were quick to respond, voting to impeach the President for high crimes and misdemeanors. In the spring of 1868 Johnson was placed on trial in the Senate, under the threat of removal from office. Fortunately for the beleaguered President, seven Republicans sided with the Democrats and managed to acquit Johnson with only one vote to spare. (The necessary two-thirds vote to remove Johnson from office was 36 votes, but the Senate voted 35 for and 19 against, with those opposing his removal consisting of seven Republicans and twelve Democrats.) After hearing the verdict, the aged Thaddeus Stevens shouted out, notes historian Remini: "The Country is going to the devil." The old House warrior died not long afterward. Johnson may have survived removal from office, but his wings remained permanently clipped. He would exert little influence on the direction of Reconstruction during the final ten months of his presidency.

2

A Mixed Record

Following the Civil War the future of the nation's blacks, including those still held as slaves, looked brighter than ever before. Lincoln's 1862 Emancipation Proclamation went into effect on New Year's Day 1863, and served as an indicator of the direction the federal government was intending to take relative to slavery. Congress, led by the Radical Republicans, had passed the Thirteenth Amendment in January, just months before the end of the war, which abolished slavery. After centuries of constant oppression and racism, blacks had every good reason to expect everything—from freedom to the vote.

BARRIERS TO ENFRANCHISEMENT

Yet some influential white Southerners chose to dig in their heels and block the tidal wave of reform in their states. During 1865 and 1866 white-dominated Southern legislatures passed the Black Codes, which placed extraordinary restrictions on black movement, freedom, and progress. Under such laws blacks were kept in segregated worlds, unable to enter many Southern stores, hotels, public restrooms, and means of transportation, such as steamboats, trains, and ferries. In Georgia, Arkansas, and Texas, schools were closed to black children longing to learn to read and write. And, above all, post-Civil War black Southerners were denied their right to vote.

Southerners made almost no attempts to cover their tracks in passing such laws. They were intent in their purposes, certain that blacks were inferior to whites and undeserving of such privileges as voting. But Northerners did not simply sit back and watch the South's black population being denied their rights. During the years between 1865 and 1869 Congress added three amendments to the Constitution, not only ending slavery, but recognizing the rights and citizenship of blacks and their enfranchisement as voters.

There were other laws passed, including one providing for the Freedmen's Bureau, sponsored by a moderate Republican senator from Illinois, Lyman Trumbull. The bureau was intended to "help freedmen obtain land; gain an education; negotiate labor contracts with white planters; settle legal and criminal disputes involving black and white people; and provide food, medical care, and transportation for black and white people left destitute by the war." Congress passed additional acts during the early years following the Civil War as well, including the Civil Rights Act of 1866 and the Reconstruction Act of 1867. The first act intended to recognize the citizenship of any person born in the United States (excluding Indians) and entitle them to their basic rights. The Reconstruction Act divided the South into five military districts under federal military control, with the intention of dismantling white-controlled state governments across the post-war South.

New Opportunities for Blacks

During the dozen years that followed the war, the period of Reconstruction, blacks not only gained the right to vote, but also served in some of the highest elected offices in the land. Throughout the 1870s hundreds of black men were

THE ELECTIONS OF 1868 AND 1872

No man emerged from the Civil War a greater hero to Northerners than General Ulysses S. Grant. The Illinois military man had repeatedly defeated Southern armies and even brought the army of General Robert E. Lee to its knees, ending the four-year-old conflict in 1865. As the presidential election of 1868 approached, Grant was the unanimous choice for the Republican nomination.

Grant was challenged by the Democratic nominee from New York, Horatio Seymour. While Grant supported Congress and Radical Reconstruction generally, the Democrats wrote up a party platform, endorsed by Seymour, that was highly critical of Congress, calling its involvement and control of Reconstruction a flagrant, even unconstitutional, grab for power.

Republicans responded by reminding the nation that the Democrats had been the party of rebellion and secession back in 1860 and throughout the Civil War. Using a tactic that, in time, became known as "waving the bloody shirt," the Republicans painted the Democrats as the cause of the Civil War and those who were struggling against Reconstruction.

In the midst of the election campaign during the fall of 1868, Ku Klux Klan members across the South launched many attacks against blacks and carpetbaggers, committing hundreds of murders. The violence may have cost Grant some votes through intimidation to Southern Republicans, but he still managed to win the popular vote, with a majority of over 300,000 votes. In the electoral vote, Grant carried a landslide of 214 votes to Seymour's 80.

During the four years of Grant's first term, he tried to push for national elected to state legislatures across the South and even to the U.S. Congress, where no black man had ever served before. Forty-one black men were elected as sheriffs; five became city mayors. In Tallahassee, Florida, and Little Rock in Arkansas, blacks became police chiefs. The days of white

healing between the North and South, as well as supporting the call for black rights and the vote. But several factors kept him from achieving his goals, and from even becoming a good president. For one thing, many white Americans were already tired of Reconstruction. Also, Grant's talents did not serve him well as President. He surrounded himself with old friends and former wartime comrades as his advisors, and some of those men became embroiled in serious scandals that tainted the Grant administration. Even when scoundrels among his advisors were uncovered, Grant sometimes continued to support them, unable to separate his personal connections from his professional duties.

By 1872, even members of Grant's own party were ready to dump him as the Republican candidate. Some left the Republican camp, formed their own political group, the Liberal Republican Party, and ran a New York newspaper editor, Horace Greeley, as their candidate. Democrats liked Greeley and hung their star on him as their own candidate. Yet most Americans remained loyal to Grant, who won a second term with 56 percent of the vote.

During his second term, Grant supported Congress's Civil Rights Act of 1875, but Reconstruction as a national policy was dying. The president rode through his last four years focusing on foreign policy, and became obsessed with annexing Santo Domingo in the Caribbean, which he thought might provide a new home for some of the South's blacks.

By 1876, Grant was interested in a third term as president, but the party bosses sidestepped him and supported Ohio Governor Rutherford B. Hayes instead. Eight years of the Grant administration had proven to be enough both for the Republicans and for most Americans.

political control and dominance across the South seemed a dim memory.

Every black Southerner was soon aware that he or she was living in a new political era. Slavery was a thing of the past and opportunities awaited. Perhaps a large number of both blacks and whites in America believed the future would swing differently for blacks, yet some of this was wishful thinking and sentimental hope, the kind expressed in a speech in 1872 by the first black associate justice of the South Carolina Supreme Court, Jonathan J. Wright. Wright had worked before and during the Civil War alongside the great black abolitionist, Frederick Douglass, to bring down slavery. Wright had a dream of America's future in which race would no longer matter:

> *Let us with a fixed, firm, hearty, earnest, and unswerving determination move steadily on and on, fanning the flame of true liberty until the last vestige of oppression shall be destroyed, and when that eventful period shall arrive, when, in the selection of rulers, both State and Federal, we shall know no North, no East, no South, no West, no white nor colored, no Democrat nor Republican, but shall choose men because of their moral and intrinsic value, their honesty and integrity, their love of unmixed liberty, and their ability to perform well the duties to be committed to their charge.*

White Racism Persists

Yet such sentiments were not shared by many white Southerners, who did not intend to surrender their political ground, or even their basic principle of race—that blacks were not equal by nature, but were inferior. Such white racism was not limited to Southern whites, but reflected an assumption held by many Northern whites, as well. Northerners may have fought for or supported bringing an end to slavery, but most were not willing to accept blacks as equals. Such a view was certainly held by the provisional governor of South Carolina, appointed by President Johnson in 1865, who wrote: "The African has been in all ages, a savage or a slave. God created him inferior to the white man in form, color, and intellect, and no legislation or culture can make him his equal."

Despite such racism, the Radical Republicans pushed their view of Reconstruction onto the former Confederate states, and some Southerners did appear to come around and accept federal guidelines and laws that recognized black rights. By 1868 nearly all of the former Rebel states had rejoined the ranks of the United States, with only three still remaining under the yoke of military control by the end of the year. The following year the Fifteenth Amendment was passed and further guarantees were made to the South's blacks. However, defiance remained a reality, with the efforts of such clandestine groups as the Ku Klux Klan constantly working to intimidate blacks from exercising their rights.

RACISM IN DISGUISE

The Ku Klux Klan was just one of the groups established across the South during the years following the end of the Civil War whose sole purpose was to intimidate blacks from claiming the rights that were theirs. Originally the Klan was little more than a veterans' organization. Confederates from Pulaski, Tennessee, established the first Klan chapter in the summer of 1866. The group was like a college fraternity, with innocent rituals and secret oaths. But after a short period of fraternal hobnobbing, the Klansmen got down to some more serious and frightening business.

Klan leaders began using their local chapters or "dens" to achieve political goals, including standing firm against the efforts of Reconstructionists. They especially despised the "progress" being made by the South's blacks. Some saw the Klan as a means of protecting their fellow whites. As historian James Roark notes, according to an early Klan organizer in Georgia, former Confederate General John B. Gordon, the Klan was immediately popular with white Southerners due to the "instinct of self-preservation . . . the sense of insecurity and danger, particularly in those neighborhoods where the Negro population largely predominated."

Intimidation and Killings

Klan members often met in secret, and wore hoods and other disguises to keep their identities unknown. Such costumes were worn also to frighten their victims. Klansmen sometimes rode at night to remote farmhouses where blacks lived and warned them not to register to vote or to challenge white authority in any way. The ways of the Klan sometimes included killing people by hanging, or simply shooting them. Blacks were beaten and sometimes whipped, just as they had been by their slave masters. There were cases involving widespread raids or assaults on black communities that ended in the killings of dozens of hapless victims.

Klansmen also intimidated others they hated, including Northerners who tried to influence Southern politics and the South's white culture. School teachers who taught black students were constant targets. Schools were burned, and teachers sometimes were dragged out and whipped. An Irish-born teacher in Cross Plains was hanged by Klansmen. An estimated 400 hangings of blacks across the South took place between 1868 and 1871, many at the hands of such terror radicals as the Ku Klux Klan.

The actions of the Klan and other such groups eventually became so violent and sinister that the federal government intervened. Congress passed a series of laws between 1870 and 1871, called the enforcement acts, that banned such ter-

A cartoon from *Harper's Weekly* magazine from 1874 commenting that harassment by the Ku Klux Klan and the White League was worse than slavery for African-Americans. The White League was effectively the military arm of the Democratic Party.

ror groups and authorized the use of the U.S. Army as a tool to combat these hate organizations. When the government intervened under these laws, arresting hundreds of Klansmen and placing them on trial, much of the Klan activity dried up. By 1872 many of those who had ridden across the darkened landscape of the South to strike terror in the hearts of innocent blacks had put away their bedsheet costumes.

CARPETBAGGERS AND SCALAWAGS

Many of the laws passed by the Radical Republicans sought to limit the political power of Southern whites, especially those who had supported the Confederacy during the Civil War. This left the way open for Northerners to make their way into the Southern states and take advantage of the power vacuum. Sometimes such Northerners were called "carpetbaggers," because they arrived carrying their clothes and other personal belongings in a common type of suitcase called a carpetbag, which was often sewed out of patterned carpet pieces. Many of the so-called carpetbaggers were former Union soldiers who had stayed in the South after the war was over. Others came down South with plans to profit from the defeated Confederacy, take control of politics, or to volunteer to aid blacks through the Freedman's Bureau or some other benevolent group, such as a church society.

Many of the carpetbaggers were hated by Southerners, who thought they were, at best, interfering and, at worst, manipulating the post-war South. Yet Southerners hated those they called "scalawags" even more. Scalawags were native-born Southerners who cooperated with Northern Reconstructionists, especially those who became members of the Republican Party. Many of the scalawags were actually white farmers, who hoped Reconstruction policies might help get them back on their feet or aid in recovering the personal or financial losses they had incurred during the war.

A Record of Achievement

One constant claim by Southerners was that those who supported the Reconstruction state governments were corrupt or incompetent; that the carpetbaggers and scalawags who represented those governments were really out for themselves. Such charges were generally unfounded. Certainly the carpetbagger governments were no more corrupt than most political systems anywhere else in America at that time.

In their defense, these new state governments, some of which supported black voting and the election of black officials, accomplished a significant record of achievement. They supported and established the first state-funded public school system open to both white and black students. They passed state and local laws designed to guarantee black rights. These laws made it illegal for such businesses as railroads, hotels and other public venues to discriminate against blacks. The Reconstruction governments fought against, and sometimes brought down, their local Black Codes. They evened out the tax code, so that it did not discriminate by race, yet southern tax rates during this era were generally high. Reconstructionists across the South, whether Northern carpetbaggers or Southern scalawags, encouraged regional economic growth and development, helped finance railroad construction, and encouraged new industries, such as lumber mills, ironworks and steel plants, factories, and textile mills across the South.

SUBVERTING THE LAW

Some white Southerners became less overt in their opposition to the advance of blacks. With national laws guaranteeing black voting, some white leaders tried to work around the laws. In 1871 state legislators in Georgia passed a law creating the first poll tax as a requirement for voting. The poll tax did not, technically, discriminate on the basis of race, as the tax was required of all voters. But the law was subversive. Many would-be black voters were too poor to pay such a tax, so they were denied the right to vote. To ensure that the poll tax did not eliminate any poor white voters, additional laws were passed, usually referred to as "grandfather clauses." Such laws stated that anyone who could not pay a poll tax could still vote if his father or grandfather had been able to vote prior to 1867. Grandfather clauses obviously applied only to whites, and not to blacks. Other laws declared that a person could be denied the right to even register to vote if one of his grandparents had been a slave.

While such laws restricted blacks officially, whites also restricted them on a street level through their business practices or social customs. A black family might be denied a room in a Southern inn or hotel simply because of their race. A storeowner might not serve blacks as his customers. Banks might not allow blacks to enter, even to deposit their own money. Schools, public transportation, churches, even cemeteries were closed to blacks. Despite changes to the Constitution and goals to support blacks politically, many Americans erected their own stumbling blocks to black progress.

THE CIVIL RIGHTS ACT OF 1875

Not to be completely undercut, during the latter days of Reconstruction the U.S. Congress took a significant step to rein in these white efforts to deny blacks their rights and privileges. Members passed the Civil Rights Act of 1875, which was sponsored by one of the longstanding supporters of black civil rights, Charles Sumner, a senator from Massachusetts. Prior to the Civil War Sumner had been an abolitionist and had received a severe beating on the Senate floor at the hands of a South Carolina House member in 1856, after speaking out against slavery. Sumner had spent his entire public career in support of ending slavery and of

SHARECROPPERS

In the South during Reconstruction, many poor families, black and white, became sharecroppers. A rich landowner assigned each family a piece of land on which they could build a small house and set up a farm. The croppers paid the owner a share of the value of their annual harvest—usually one third or one half of the total. The croppers were provided with tools and livestock by the owner, and they bought food, clothing, seeds, and fertilizer from a local merchant or plantation store.

Some sharecroppers were able to buy their own farm animals and equipment and became permanent tenants on the land.

black equality. He was one of the few Northerners to give early support to integration in public schools. Unfortunately, Sumner died in 1874 before the passage of the new civil rights legislation.

The intention of the Civil Rights Act of 1875 was to fill in the gaps that had been overlooked by the Civil Rights Act of 1866. The new act stated:

> *All persons… shall be entitled to the full and equal enjoyment of the accommodations, advantages, facilities, and privileges of inns, public conveyances on land or water, theaters, and other places of public amusement.*

The act was well intended and included some of the best ideals the U.S. government could guarantee. And it was one of the last pieces of Reconstruction legislation. For more than a decade, Congress had worked to protect blacks across the South. But Americans were now tired of Reconstruction. Many of the Southern states had been readmitted back into the Union, and it seemed to many people that there was nothing left to do to protect the South's former slaves.

LAST DAYS OF RECONSTRUCTION

The Grant administration had served as a significant supporter of Congress-driven Reconstruction, unlike President Johnson. President Grant fought against the tactics of the Ku Klux Klan and he signed off on significant pieces of Reconstruction legislation. But Reconstruction began to change during the 1870s. Some of the old leaders of the Radical Republicans were dying off—Thaddeus Stevens died in 1868, and Charles Sumner six years later.

The cost of some of the elements of Reconstruction, including keeping federal troops across the South, was a constant drain on the government. New schools may have been established in the former Confederate states, instituted for blacks and whites alike, but these schools cost money, and many Americans began to resent higher taxes to pay for such "progress." Other Reconstruction programs also cost money and some were beginning to come under fire because of corruption.

Following Grant's reelection in 1872 the United States fell into a significant depression in 1873, drawing away the attention of many Americans from Reconstruction. Also, the Grant administration itself proved corrupt. Although Grant himself remained an honest president, a number of federal officials under him took bribes and favors from special interest groups and big businessmen. Given such distractions, Reconstruction began to take a second or even third seat in the minds of many Americans across the North.

A New President

The final fate of Reconstruction was decided by the election of 1876. Grant was not accepted for a third term by the Republican Party, which chose, instead, Rutherford B. Hayes, a Civil War veteran and politician from Ohio. The Democrats chose a New York reformer, named Samuel J. Tilden. Although the election became controversial, with disputed ballots in four states, Hayes still emerged as the winning candidate. During the controversies of the election, Democrats agreed to allow Hayes to take the presidency in exchange for the Republicans' promise to end Reconstruction as quickly as possible. Hayes had nothing to do with the agreement between Republicans and Democrats, but he wasted no time in bringing Reconstruction to an official end when he took office in the spring of 1877.

By then Reconstruction had largely rolled off the rails. There had been important successes, without question, as Northerners and cooperative Southerners had helped newly freed slaves to find direction in their lives, while protecting them as they could. A new school system had come into place, one much more extensive and comprehensive, and designed for students of both races. But Reconstruction had not fixed every problem in the post-war South. Few blacks gained significant property and many were still living as second- or third-class citizens.

One reason for some of the failures of Reconstruction was that many Americans, both Northerners and Southerners, never bought into it. Only the most idealistic Radical Republicans, and those motivated by reform ideals or their view of Christian charity, actually gave their strong support to the goals of Reconstruction. But the South still emerged as a region that had experienced great change. Through the Civil War, the Emancipation Proclamation, amendments that destroyed slavery and guaranteed black rights, and Reconstruction itself, Southerners had gone through one of the most trying eras in their history. And, with the approach of the 1880s and 1890s, more change was on its way.

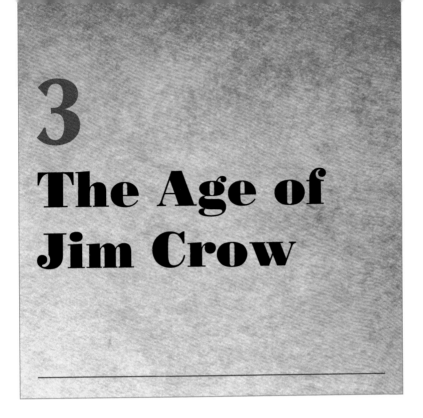

3

The Age of Jim Crow

With the end of Reconstruction, officially in 1877, many of the hopes of blacks across the South died. For more than a decade promises had been made to African Americans, who had finally been allowed to rise above the struggles and humiliations of slavery as new opportunities appeared on the horizon. But the opportunities remained unattainable for many blacks, as white apathy and racism finally brushed aside the goals of Reconstruction. The intentions of the Thirteenth, Fourteenth, and Fifteenth Amendments almost rang hollow for many Southern blacks.

POSTPONING EQUALITY

Throughout the years from 1875 to 1900 black people across the South were slowly but certainly denied their basic rights. The possibility of equality before the law blew away like dust. Black politicians who had gained their public offices during the 1860s and early 70s were now stripped of their seats and excluded from politics. Many blacks found themselves confined to menial jobs and viewed by whites as second-class citizens. Laws were passed by white legislatures that were purposefully unfriendly to blacks. Blacks who did not cooperate with this redirection of public life in America might risk a beating or even hanging, a practice known during this era as lynching. So much that blacks had gained, or at least had been promised, during Reconstruction was lost.

Segregation was the new social norm between the black and white races by the early 1880s. Almost every element of life in the South hinged on keeping the two races apart, and the same could also be said for many parts of the North during those same years. Black children might be able to go to school, a privilege not generally available in the South before the Civil War, but in most places such schools were attended by blacks only. Blacks were put aside at nearly every turn, kept from public places where whites could be found, or relegated to the balconies of theaters, the back seats of churches, and to completely separate railroad cars.

Then, in 1883, the United States Supreme Court dealt a harsh blow to blacks, one that represented a giant step backward from goals already attained during Reconstruction. That year the Court declared the Civil Rights Act of 1875 to be unconstitutional. The Court stated that the act could only ban discrimination on the part of state governments, not at the hands of individuals. The Civil Rights Act had rendered it illegal for hotel owners, steamboat operators, or any other person operating a "public conveyance," or lodging "accommodation," or "place of public amusement" to discriminate on the basis of race. Now, with the Court's new ruling, it became perfectly legal for innkeepers, steamboat companies, theater owners, or railroad operators to discriminate against blacks, so long as state law did not force such private citizens to practice segregation.

AT EVERY TURN, A BARRIER

Segregation seemed to know no bounds. It did not come on all at once, but in pieces, bit by bit. Even as late as 1885 a black attorney from the North, T. McCants Stewart, made a trip to Columbia, South Carolina, and found little discrimination or segregation. He wrote later to his fellow New Yorkers even of how pleasant he had found his visit to the South, stating, as historian Darlene Hine notes:

> *I can ride in first class cars on the railroads and in the streets. I can go into saloons and get refreshments even as in New York. I can stop in and drink a glass of soda and be more politely waited upon than in some parts of New England.*

But the black lawyer from New York City had made his tour of the South Carolina city before most segregation legislation became law in that state. Even the word "segregation" itself was virtually unknown in the South until the early years of the twentieth century.

It was not that, prior to segregation laws, blacks and whites had socialized in every way together or had completely shared common experiences. They might have done so, of course, but they did not. Prior to the days of legislated segregation, there were plenty of examples of blacks and whites attending the same public political rallies, or county fairs, or town fish fries, or Fourth of July bashes. But even on those occasions, the blacks and whites who attended might not have interacted that much, if at all, with members of the other race. And when they did interact, it was assumed, all across the South, that whites were free to address blacks in any way they chose, while blacks had to follow strict expectations of behavior. What would be extremely different by the 1890s was that state law typically came to *require* segregation between the races.

DAYS OF JIM CROW

The segregation that fell into practice during the final years of the 1800s even had a name: "Jim Crow." This term dated back to the days of popular musical performances, in which white performers had blackened their faces to mimic black singers and dancers. During the 1830s and 1840s the white performer, Thomas "Daddy" Rice, sang and pantomimed a routine called "Jump Jim Crow." His popular act included over-exaggerated gestures and dance steps to simulate a stereotype of African-American performances. It is not certain just how Rice's performance and song became the source of

LYNCHING THE REACH OF VIOLENCE

As the roots of Jim Crowism grew deeper, the level of violence against blacks across the South expanded to new extremes. Lynching was commonplace across the South by the 1890s, and was used as an extreme form of intimidation. Between 1889 and 1932 approximately 3,750 people were lynched in America—an average of two or three people each week for 30 years. Most of these hangings took place in the South, and the vast majority of the victims were black.

Lynchings were almost always carried out by white mobs, who attacked their black victims for a variety of "reasons." Commonly, whites justified lynching a black man because of his allegedly having raped a white woman, but many lynchings occurred when a group of whites simply lost control. Historian Darlene Hine notes an editorial in the newspaper, *The Atlanta Constitution*, that stated: "There are places and occasions when the natural fury of men cannot be restrained by all the laws of Christendom." Sometimes lynching victims were black men who had done nothing but achieve economically, or who had allegedly offended whites by their "unacceptable" behavior. Such behavior might have been nothing more than smiling at a white woman.

the label for the political segregation of the late nineteenth century, but the connection was made and was popularized.

Jim Crow laws, then, were legislation passed by Southern states to force or require segregation in nearly all aspects of life for blacks and whites. Such laws fit the white racist view of black inferiority. After all, if blacks were inferior, why should whites tolerate their presence at public gatherings, storefronts and other businesses, or such entertainment venues as theaters or amusement parks? There was a resentment on the part of many whites when they had to share their experiences with blacks. Sometimes, blacks could accept being denied access by establishing an alternative for themselves. If a white church would not accept them, blacks could establish their own congregation. If they were unwanted as members of a white organization, blacks might manage to create a similar club or group with exclusively black membership. And if they were turned away from white theaters, they could set up their own entertainment houses.

RIDING SEPARATELY

By the 1890s one serious sticking point between blacks and whites focused on railroad transportation. Some whites did not want to travel in the same first-class passenger coaches on railroads as black passengers. Increasingly, laws were passed throughout Southern states denying blacks the right to purchase tickets for a first-class rail car. Prior to such restrictive laws, it was common practice across the South for railroad conductors, and sometimes the white passengers themselves, to keep blacks from riding in first-class cars, even if they had purchased a first-class ticket. Blacks were frequently forced to ride in second-class coaches, which were often included on trains as the smoking cars, where smokers could puff away on their cigars, pipes, and cigarettes. Smoking cars were usually placed at the front of trains, just

A classroom scene inside a segregated school for blacks in New York City in about 1870. Such schools were invariably anything but equal to those for white children. Teachers were poorly trained, if at all, and books and writing materials were in short supply.

behind the locomotive, so they were dirty from the engine smoke, not to mention the smokers inside the car.

The examples of such treatment against blacks were many. In 1889 a group of black Baptists from Savannah, Georgia, paid for their first-class tickets to ride a train to a religious convention in Indiana. Word reached a station up the line and, when the train made a stop, the black passengers were threatened by a mob of angry whites. One white man pulled a handgun, pointed it straight at a frightened, screaming black woman and threatened to blow her brains out if she did not quiet down and get off the train.

Texas passed one of the first "separate car laws" in the South as early as 1865, with Mississippi following suit just three years later. Ironically, the first of these laws had been established in Massachusetts—a Northern state—in 1841, 20 years before the Civil War. Massachusetts had then been one of the most important antislavery states. Such laws now became common across the South, with little variation between them. Then, in 1885, Tennessee passed its separate car law, but added a unique phrase to the equation. The Tennessee law was based on the concept of "separate but equal." Separate rail cars, yes, but so what? Blacks were being promised that the cars they were to ride in would be as nice, comfortable, and accommodating as the cars reserved for whites. Florida passed a similar law two years later. In general, the railroads did not like separate car laws, because they cost them money—the railways often had to run extra cars on their trains to accommodate blacks and whites separately.

PLESSY V. FERGUSON

In 1891 Louisiana lawmakers passed a statewide separate car law—just one more of the many segregation laws passed by a white-dominated state legislature. The law was clear, straightforward, and prejudicial:

All railway companies carrying passengers in their coaches in this state shall provide equal but separate accommodations for the white, and colored races, by providing two or more passenger coaches for each train. No person or persons shall be permitted to occupy seats in coaches, other than the ones assigned to them, on account of the race they belong to.

The law was binding not only on blacks, but also on the railroad officials and train conductors who had to enforce the law directly. Anyone who violated the Louisiana law risked a $25 fine and 20 days in jail.

Segregation on public means of transportation was not new to Louisiana or New Orleans in the early 1890s. Back in 1867 streetcars had been segregated by law in New Orleans. One out of every three streetcars was marked with a large black star, which indicated that it was to be used by black passengers. Whites, however, could board such cars if it was convenient for them. Only blacks who had served as Union soldiers could ride in the whites-only streetcars. But protests and defiance by blacks in the city had caused New Orleans' streetcar companies to eliminate the stars that designated cars for blacks.

A Challenge to Segregated Transport

Now, a generation later, another public transportation segregation law had been passed. Soon a local group, called the Citizens' Committee to Test the Constitutionality of the Separate Car Law, decided to challenge their state's separate car law. Its members came from a variety of professions, including teachers, businessmen, attorneys, former Union soldiers, government bureaucrats, and social activists. They wanted to create a test case that could make its way into the state court system, and, hopefully, bring about a decision that declared the separate car law illegal.

When setting up their challenge to the law, the committee decided to pick a person who was only technically "black," someone who was light skinned enough to "pass" for a white man. In doing so, the committee hoped to show how absurd the law was to enforce. In 1892 they selected a shoemaker from New Orleans in his late twenties, named Homer A. Plessy. Plessy's ancestors had included both blacks and whites. He was an octoroon—a person who was only one-eighth black by lineage—and was so light skinned that he was constantly taken to be white. Before the committee sent Plessy to buy a first-class ticket on the East Louisiana Raiload, members informed the targeted rail line of what they were about to do. Railroad officials were happy to cooperate.

On the designated day, a muggy June 7, the New Orleans shoemaker entered the Press Street Station and purchased a first-class ticket for the train. No one questioned him when he made the purchase for, to anyone standing around watching, Plessy was just another white man buying a ticket. He boarded the Number Eight Train's whites-only car and took his seat. The train pulled out and headed down the tracks. After several minutes, Plessy summoned the train conductor, J. J. Dowling, and informed him that he was black. Historian Harvey Fireside recalls Plessy's words to Dowling: "I have to tell you that according to Louisiana law, I am a colored man." Soon, Plessy was arrested for violating the state's separate car law.

A Verdict in the Supreme Court

The case—known as *Plessy v. Ferguson* for the name of the judge who first heard the case—wound its way through the Louisiana court system, until it finally landed before the United States Supreme Court. Attorneys for Plessy argued that the Louisiana separate car law violated the Fourteenth

Amendment, since it denied their client his equal protection under the law. However the year was 1896 and racism was simply a part of the social landscape that nearly everyone took for granted. The Court decided against Plessy, with a vote of 8–1. Writing the majority opinion, Justice Henry Brown stated that separation of the races, as with a separate set of passenger cars on a train, did not automatically violate Plessy's rights. He could, after all, ride the train, but in a separate car.

Brown also argued that just because the races were kept separate on Louisiana's trains did not directly imply that Plessy or any other black passenger was inferior. Only Justice John Marshall Harlan, whose father had owned slaves years earlier, sided with Plessy, arguing, notes historian Harvey Fireside, that the Separate Car Act in Louisiana represented an attempt by the state to regulate "the use of a public highway by citizens of the United States solely upon the basis of race." He went on to state, speaking of the Separate Car Law: "Every one knows [that the law was created] not so much to exclude white persons from railroad cars occupied by blacks, as to exclude colored people from coaches . . . assigned to white persons."

Aftermath of the Case

The *Plessy v. Ferguson* decision represented one of the most important Supreme Court cases in the history of the United States. It knocked the wind out of the sails of the Fourteenth Amendment, making it nearly useless in cases involving segregation and "separate but equal." More Jim Crowism followed. Eight Southern states had passed separate car laws before the *Plessy* decision, but five others joined their ranks over the next 15 years. New Jim Crow laws filled the statute books, segregating drinking fountains and public toilets and banning blacks from whites-only lunch counters and restaurants. All Southern states, from Maryland to Texas, passed Jim Crow laws throughout the 1890s and into the twentieth century. Many Southern courtrooms kept at least two Bibles on hand, one to be used by white witnesses and the other by blacks, on which they were "to swear to tell the truth." Alabama even made it a crime for blacks and whites to play checkers together.

Life changed for the vast majority of the nation's eight million blacks following the *Plessy v. Ferguson* decision, and it did so for the worse. Long after the case itself, ripples of the decision would cause other millions of blacks, yet unborn, to struggle under the Supreme Court's establishment and legitimizing of "separate but equal" on a national scale. The concept would remain the law of the land for more than half a century.

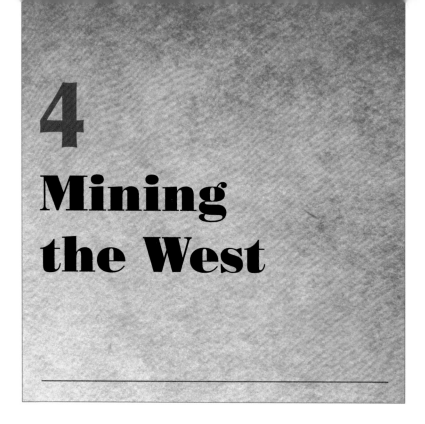

4
Mining the West

In the aftermath of the Civil War, the gaze of thousands, even millions, of Americans and foreign immigrants—Europeans, Chinese, and others—turned to the untamed West. They were cattleman and cowboys, farmers and settlers, and prospectors and miners. Before the end of the 1800s, these groups of restless entrepreneurs and adventurers would leave their mark on lands stretching from the treeless Plains westward to the shining mountains of the Rockies.

GOLD SEEKERS

Prior to 1850 Americans had simply moved incrementally across the landscape, beginning along the Atlantic seaboard in the 1600s. With each passing generation, people had moved a little further westward, leeching their way across the continent, and slowly filling in the landscape. By the early 1840s American settlement had reached the tier of states just west of the Mississippi River. The furthest point of emigration had made its way to Texas.

Once gold was announced for the taking in California, Americans suddenly leaped across the continent, leaving much of the Great Plains and intermountain region still open for settlement. California gold inspired the imagination of a generation of prospectors. The new pattern of settlement, brought about by the discovery of precious metals in the West, would be to create isolated pockets of settlement in places where the intrepid and adventurous hoped to strike it rich. From the 1850s to the 1890s gold seekers rattled around the West, seeking their fortunes in such remote locales as Washoe, Nevada; Butte, Montana; Tombstone, Arizona; Cripple Creek, Colorado; and the Black Hills of the Dakota Territory.

A MOUNTAIN OF GOLD AND SILVER

Following the discovery of gold in northern California in 1848, one of the first significant "gold" strike sites in the West was located just a few hundred miles (km) to the southeast, in the Washoe Mountains of today's Nevada, which lie in the Great Basin, east of the Sierra Nevadas. The first Anglo-Americans to discover gold there were not actual prospectors, but Mormons who stumbled across a heavy vein of gold locked in quartz. When the discovery tapped out the Mormons left, only to have their places taken up by gold seekers from California and elsewhere who had heard rumors of the original strike. Significant strikes eluded these eager diggers until 1859, when a pair of Irishmen, Peter O'Riley and Patrick McLaughlin, finally hit "pay dirt," soil that contains valuable metals, in a draw (water drainage valley) later known as "Gold Canyon."

That summer the two prospectors and a few others in the region began extracting large quantities of a strange dirt.

The ore samples were 75 percent silver and 25 percent gold, worth $3,876 per ton at that time. O'Riley and McLaughlin had made a valuable strike, later known as the Ophir Mine. In the meantime a third prospector, Canadian-born Henry T. P. Comstock, had stepped forward and talked his way into a partnership with the two Irishmen, claiming he owned the local spring they had been using. In time, the lucrative mine became known as the Comstock Lode.

Soon the Washoe Mountains were crawling with prospectors. The Comstock Lode proved to be a mountain of silver, and mining operations were scattered across the region. By 1860 the frontier town of Virginia City was home to 10,000 miners, whose claims and camps hugged the mountain.

THE MINING CAMPS

Nearly everyone with a stake in a western mining camp was male. Many had wives and children who remained back home to run the family farm or other business, while the husband and father took off for the diggings. A small number of prospectors brought along their wives, who soon found themselves popular in the camps for a variety of reasons. One miner's wife opened up a makeshift dining hall and, by nightfall, was feeding 20 miners, each paying her a dollar. Ultimately she made more money cooking than her husband made prospecting.

There was a tremendous amount of "come and go" in the mining camps, depending on how well a mining region produced valuable metals. Western miners, in fact, were perhaps the most mobile group in American history, with the typical prospector ready to pack up his tools and belongings at the slightest rumor of a gold strike elsewhere. One California mining community of 100 prospectors in 1850 could only boast five of the same men still working the local diggings in 1856. Thirty thousand men abandoned the camps in

California in 1858 on the rumor of a discovery of gold along the Fraser River in British Columbia. Henry Comstock himself, despite having a virtual mountain of silver named after him in Nevada, sold one of his claims for $11,000 and

A mountainside in the Rockies is honeycombed with silver mines, as pictured in this contemporary wood engraving. Miners used shovels, picks, and drills to dig tunnels in the rock. They used wooden supports to keep the tunnels from collapsing.

another for two mules, then lit out for diggings that took him from Oregon to Idaho to Montana. Comstock lost all his money in bad investments, and, 11 years after the discovery of the lode that bore his name, finally shot himself.

MULTICULTURAL MINERS

The lure of gold and silver in the West knew no human bounds. People from all sorts of backgrounds, points of origin, and ethnicities made their way into the mining camps, all hungry for the precious metals they had heard stories about. Mining camps became cosmopolitan places, where miners of every stripe rubbed shoulders. Men from the East, sometimes called "tenderfeet" by westerners, worked alongside Californians called "yonsiders." There were the educated and the illiterate, those already rich, and those who wanted to become rich. There were former slaves and former Confederates.

Many of the miners were Americans, of course, but others came from around the world, including China and Hawaii. Mexicans came in abundance to some mining regions, sometimes bringing their skills from experience working mines south of the border.

European arrivals included men from the British Isles—Englishmen, Irish lads, Welsh workers, Scots, and Cornish miners, often called "Cousin Jacks." Continental Europeans included French, Russians, and German Jews.

Sometimes the miners brought vestiges of their native cultures with them, helping to create unique worlds in the West. Many western mining towns had their French influences, such as a local *Café de Paris*. So many Germans were working in mines around Denver by 1860 that the mining town had its own German newspaper. English miners sometimes played cricket matches on lazy Sunday afternoons. Many camps had a Chinese laundry, where smart-minded, hard-working men from China sometimes made more money with soap and water than miners made with their picks and shovels.

Virginia City

The silver and gold boom centered on Virginia City proved gigantic and paid out in the millions. Between 1859 and 1865 miners tapping the Comstock Lode unearthed $50 million worth of gold and silver. Ultimately 16 great strikes, or "bonanzas," were discovered. The largest, the "Big Bonanza," was uncovered in October 1873, from diggings that extended 1,000 feet (300 meters) into the earth. By this time the days of surface prospecting were past, having been replaced by corporate mining operations, which provided the capital investment to excavate thousands of feet underground. One miner described the Big Bonanza's silver vein as so large, notes historian C. Spence, that "a blind man driving a four-horse team could have followed it in a snowstorm." The vein proved to be more than 50 feet (15 m) in width!

By the mid-1870s Virginia City was a burgeoning frontier city of 20,000 residents, where German, Irish, Cornish (from Britain's Cornwall region), and Mexican miners labored in the hot underground mine shafts by the hundreds. Between 1859 and 1882 the Comstock Lode produced more than $300 million worth of silver and gold. The Comstock mining operations had also managed to redefine mining itself, as the region's valuable ores proved to be located as far underground as 2,100 feet (640 m)—deeper than any mines existing at that time. New heavy timbering methods had to be developed and new types of heavy equipment introduced.

COLORADO ORES

At the time of the discovery of the Comstock Lode, miners were hearing of another series of strikes out in the Colorado Rockies. In the summer of 1858, claims of gold were issuing out of the Pike's Peak area, which led 100,000 "Fifty-Niners" (named for the year they came) into the region. The actual strikes were located closer to modern-day Denver, more than 50 miles (80 km) to the north. The previous spring, a pair of prospectors, Captain John Beck and W. Green Russell, led a group of would-be miners into the region, where they panned for gold along the Front Range of the Rockies. Along Cherry Creek, the party hit pay dirt. Many Americans from the East chose to prospect in Colorado rather than the Nevada region, since it was up to 700 miles (1,100 km) closer. At the confluence of Cherry Creek and the South Platte River, prospectors established the settlement of Denver, named after the governor of Kansas Territory, James William Denver.

By the summer of 1859, though, half of those who had found their way into Colorado to look for gold had gone bust, finding little to justify the earlier claims of metallic wealth for the taking. Of those who remained, several did make significant gold strikes along Clear Creek. These gave rise to the mining town of Central City, where 5,000 prospectors gathered looking for the precious metal. West of Central City gold was uncovered along Gregory Gulch. Yet, during the years of prospecting between 1858 and 1868 the amount of gold, silver, and lead unearthed in this region was paltry compared to the Comstock Lode, perhaps only amounting to around $25 million.

Those who remained in the region as late as the 1870s had to rely, as did miners in Nevada, on expanded corporate mining, finding larger deposits of metal deep underground, at sites including Leadville and Durango. Leadville was a mere collection of log shacks in the late 1870s, and only became a prosperous mountain town of 14,000 residents in the early 1880s, when hardrock miners began unearthing ores of silver, lead, copper, and zinc. In 1890 perhaps the most significant gold discovery was made at Cripple Creek, Colorado, where an area of just 6 square miles (15 sq km) became dotted with 475 mines, which extracted a third of a billion dollars of gold during the quarter century leading up to World War I.

Mining brought Anglo-Americans into today's Colorado by the thousands, and changed the region's history. Originally part of the Kansas Territory, the Colorado Territory was created in 1861, and statehood followed in 1876, the United States' centennial year.

ANOTHER VIRGINIA CITY

Western prospectors were drawn by other gold and silver strikes during the late 1850s, including one in Arizona, around the old Mexican mining village of Tucson, followed by finds at Prescott in 1862. While such strikes were limited, and proved more important for discoveries of copper rather than gold, the Arizona Rush resulted in the separation of Arizona from New Mexico in 1863.

Elsewhere, another rush was soon centered along the Clearwater River in modern-day Idaho, where gold was discovered in 1860. By 1861, miners gathered along nearby Snake River into gold camps named Oro Fino and Pierce City. An immediate complication was that this territory was considered Indian Country, so the federal government was pushed to negotiate new treaties with the region's Indian nations during the summer of 1863. In 1862 gold was discovered to the south, along the Boise River Basin.

News of these findings caused many prospectors to abandon their diggings in Colorado and move north to Idaho, where they found gold along Grasshopper Creek. The rush in that region continued through the Civil War. Bannack City was established as an important mining settlement in today's Montana, followed by the founding of another mining village named Virginia City in 1863. The next year strikes were made at local sites called Last Chance Gulch and Silver Bow, today the Montana cities of Helena and Butte.

The diggings around Butte panned out the best. Originally prospectors made discoveries of gold, which they raked off the surface of the land, but other metals tapped later proved

Stagecoaches stop at Wells Fargo & Co.'s office in Virginia City, Nevada, in about 1866. Wells Fargo established itself as the leading banking and overland mail company for mining communities.

more important. A large hill of metals was unearthed, leading to the extraction of more than $2 billion worth of copper, silver, gold, and zinc. The region remains a mining center even today. Some of the era's mines were deep, similar to Colorado and Nevada, extending underground to a depth of nearly a mile (1.6 km). While such mining made fortunes for a handful of people, the overall result was that Montana became a territory in 1864 and gained statehood by 1890, along with neighboring Wyoming, where gold had been discovered along South Pass in 1867.

But there was always a human cost to calculate in these western mining operations. Companies did little to help ensure the safety of their workers, whether under or above ground. Mines were dangerous and dirty places, not to mention unhealthy. With machines drilling into mine walls in search of precious metals, miners were exposed to microscopic materials that could cause them to develop deadly silicosis. In the mines at Butte, where miners toiled at depths of 4,000 feet (1,200 m) underground and worked in close proximity to heavy equipment, a man was killed or maimed almost daily during the 1890s.

PROSPECTING METHODS

Western "prospecting" was a different kind of work to that of the hardrock miner, who labored deep underground in the employ of a well-funded mining corporation. The pattern was repeated across the West: An initial discovery of gold would bring a deluge of prospectors, most of them on their own, armed with the simplest of tools—a pick, shovel, and pan. Such men engaged in a type of prospecting called "placer mining," which wasn't really mining at all. Placer (rhymes with "passer") mining involved looking for gold through a variety of methods involving water washing. The most common and simplest was the gold pan—a flattish, wide-brimmed pan, which a prospector used to scoop up gravel from a stream bottom. Using centripetal force, he would swirl the pan in a circular motion, allowing the water and lighter rock material to slip over the edge of the pan. This would leave the heavier metal material behind, which might include gold dust, flakes, or even nuggets.

An average prospector, armed with a gold pan, squatting in a cold western mountain stream, might work through 50 panfuls of rocky and sandy material in a day's work. If each pan produced 10 cents worth of gold, he might be able to cover the inflated costs of his needs to survive in the typical mining camp. If he was working rich diggings, he might scoop up $50 worth of gold in a single pan. Legends were told of a single pan yielding as much as $1,000 of glittery metal.

Other placer methods were more complicated. The cradle, for example, involved washing shoveled ore through a sieve at the top of a cradle-like contraption and along a slanted surface featuring slats, or cleats, designed to catch the heavier gold material. A more involved method—the "Long Tom"— was an extended wooden trough built to allow a constant flow of water, with cleats again running perpendicular to the trough to catch the heavier gold. Such methods were common and well suited to frontier prospecting camps. They were simple to construct and use, and required no expensive or elaborate equipment, smelting or refining, as the gold often was found in a pure form. Such surface mining, if the prospector was fortunate, produced gold nuggets, flakes, and dust, which he often kept in a leather pouch. Sometimes gold dust was collected on the insides of goose quills.

MINING AS BIG BUSINESS

A more complex type of operation was called lode mining. Prospectors knew that the presence of gold in a streambed generally indicated the presence of a lode or vein of quartz containing gold. Miners, then, knew to look upstream from placer gold finds. Such work usually required the prospector to dig deeper into the ground than he would to placer mine. When a promising lode was unearthed, the prospector faced the problem of extracting gold locked in deposits of quartz. This process usually required the use of heavier equipment and machinery, such as stamping mills designed to pulverize the quartz. Once the quartz was broken up, the gold was removed, or extracted, with chemicals. Mercury was almost universally used, since it bonded well with gold, creating an amalgam. The amalgam material was then processed to recover the gold.

So much equipment was required at a large mining site that the cost might climb to as high as $200,000. And so much mercury was needed for gold amalgamation, that a ready source was required. In 1845 such a source was discovered—the New Almaden mine south of San Francisco in the San Jose Valley, which became one of the largest mercury mines in the world. All considered, lode mining was a complicated and expensive process.

Adding to the expense was the location of much of the gold and silver in the West, which was deep underground. Such mining required lots of digging, sometimes creating vast tunnel systems, with horizontal shafts supported by heavy, squared-off wooden beams, which required thousands of board feet of timber. By the 1880s shafts at the Comstock mines were extending down to a depth of some 3,000 feet (900 m), a distance of more than a half-mile. Steam-powered drills were brought in, often at great expense, since many mining operations were remotely located. Money had to be spent on necessary ventilating systems. An elaborate western mining operation might involve interconnected mine shafts totaling nearly 200 miles (320 km) in length.

WASHING OUT A MOUNTAIN

One additional technique, later adapted to the removal of precious metals in the West, was a dramatically different version of the placer method—hydraulic mining. This method was first utilized in 1852, when a miner named Anthony Chabot dammed a northern California stream to create a reservoir of water, then used gravity and a canvas hose to blast water into a hard stream, which washed soil from an exposure of rock and earth into a natural ditch. Stopping the flow of water occasionally, Chabot would examine the stream for gold in his natural "sluice". Making later changes to his system with the help of a couple of new partners, Chabot had invented hydraulic mining, an extremely destructive means of surface mining. Gone were the heavy timber shafts and underground tunnels. Later hoses were enlarged, leading to an 1870 model called the "Little Giant" with an opening the size of a Civil War cannon.

Within four or five years of Chabot's initial experiment, hydraulic mining sites were scattered across the West. One company's operation, the North Bloomfield Gravel Mining Company, required 1 million gallons (4.5 million liters) of water a day. Its destructive work ran around the clock, with light provided by immense fires of burning pine pitch, until electric lights were strung up in 1879. By that time nine companies were mining 1,000 miles (1,600 km) of washed out western ditches, each relying on giant nozzled hoses. Such operations were extremely wasteful, creating permanent scars on the landscape, while polluting major river systems.

EFFECTS OF MINING

But for all its excesses, western mining created one more foothold for the advance of the settling of the American West. And its output was staggering. The amounts of gold, silver, and other metals extracted from these mining operations during the second half of the nineteenth century, according to historian Robert Hine, "dwarfed all previous mining, not only in the United States but worldwide." In California alone, during 1848 and 1849, 76 tons (69 metric tons) of gold were discovered, according to federal records—more than twice the amount uncovered during the previous 60 years. The discovery of the Comstock Lode alone produced millions of ounces of silver, whereas silver production in America could previously be counted in the thousands of ounces. During the three years following the 1848 discovery of gold at Sutter's Ranch in California, the number of gold coins in circulation in America increased 20 times over, greatly expanding the nation's money supply. In the long run, the high level of gold and silver extracted from western mines caused the value of gold and silver coins to decrease, causing a severe depression across the United States by the early 1890s.

In addition, western mining made its contribution to the expansion of American industry and of capital investment in the West, while providing thousands of jobs. Perhaps most importantly, though, the mining of the West's precious metals provided an economic base in the region, which resulted in hundreds of mining camp settlements, some of which survived to become major urban centers, including Denver, San Francisco, and others.

5
Cattle and Cowboys

In 1865, the year the Civil War ended, the state of Texas was home to perhaps 5 million head of free-ranging cattle, most of them descended from Spanish breeds, and the majority consisting of lean, ornery longhorns. During the 20 years that followed, Americans—including whites, blacks, Hispanics, Indians, and others—began rounding up herds of hundreds, even thousands, of these hoofed animals and driving them north to various railheads, where they could be shipped to market. By doing this, these nineteenth-century "cowboys" created one of America's most enduring and romantic eras, even as they altered forever the eating habits of the country.

EARLY CATTLEMEN

While North America had been home to vast bison (popularly known as buffalo) herds for thousands of years, it was the Spanish who first introduced cattle to the New World, along with their longstanding tradition of herding them on the open range with men on horseback, known as *vaqueros*. A secondary influence probably came from slaves imported to the Americas, who had herded cattle back in Africa. When Spanish colonizers reached North America in the seventeenth century, cattle soon found their place across the southern Great Plains and as far afield as southern California. In time, large herds were formed or came into being through natural increase, great masses of cattle that became known as Texas Longhorns. As the Spanish, and later Mexican, cattlemen allowed their cattle to roam free, it was easy for some animals to wander off and gather in distant herds, untended by humans. These became free herds that multiplied into the millions.

A Spanish Role Model

As for those vaqueros, they became the prototype for the American cowboy of the nineteenth century. Americans first saw these Hispanic cowboys in action in Louisiana, before the region became U.S. territory. Everything the vaquero wore—including chaps, leather vest, wide-brimmed hat, kerchief, spurs, and boots—became the accepted costume of the American cowboy. Such was the influence of the vaquero that many of the words he used to describe the tools of his trade—lariat, lasso, rodeo, rancho, chaps—were also used by his American alter ego.

As long as the lands of the free-ranging longhorn herds remained in Spanish or Mexican hands, the world of the cowboy remained, largely, the world of the vaquero. But following the Texas Revolution of the 1830s and the shift of Texas to American domination, the Anglo-American cowboy became the new standard. Prior to the 1850s American cattlemen typically drove their cattle overland to markets in Shreveport or New Orleans, or perhaps a little further north.

By the late 1850s a reasonably sized market for Texas beef was established in Kansas City.

A MARKET FOR BEEF

It was the Civil War, however, that delivered the next significant change in the American cattle industry. The war created a significant market for beef to feed soldiers on both sides. The war also nearly destroyed the export markets flowing out of New Orleans, which took several years to recover afterward. This caused Texas cattlemen to point their cattle herds to markets in Missouri, Kansas, and destinations even further west by the 1870s and 1880s. The advance of the railroad also facilitated this redirecting of cattle drives northwards. Frontier towns such as Sedalia, Missouri, and the Kansas towns of Wichita, Ellsworth, Abilene, and the legendary Dodge City now became rail centers and viable cattle market towns. The first significant year of the cattle drives into Missouri was 1866, when Texas cattlemen drove more than a quarter million head to Sedalia and other Missouri destinations.

Meat Packing Plants

Another important innovation that encouraged cattle drives from Texas into Kansas was the development of meat packing plants in the Midwest. A pair of meat packers out of Chicago, Philip Armour and Gustavus Swift, turned away from the traditional practice of driving live cattle to eastern slaughterhouses, and decided instead to set up shop in such towns as Omaha and Kansas City. There large cattle pens, or stockyards, were constructed to hold huge herds of cattle. They temporarily housed about 120,000 cattle in some years. Workers butchered the animals, dressed them into sides of beef on "disassembly" lines and then shipped the meat to eastern markets in the era's new refrigerated rail cars.

Since meat only represented about 50 percent of a steer's standing weight, this new method of shipping to market cut costs dramatically. The meat packers could also make additional profits on the parts of the animals that had previously been underutilized or even discarded. Dried blood could be turned into fertilizer, hooves into glue, animal fat into a butter substitute, and even the bones could be made into knife handles. Under this new system, meat packers actually made more money from these "by-products" than they did from the sale of the meat itself. Much of the rest of the animal was ground up into a indistinct material that became some form of sausage or potted meat product.

All this—the post-Civil War demand, the western advance of the railroads, changes in cattle processing and shipping logistics, markets for secondary animal products—translated into high profit potentials for cattlemen in Texas. Some kept their own herds; others could easily round up free-ranging cattle, or even purchase cattle for $5 or $10 a head from a ranch in Mexico (some Texans simply stole Mexican cattle, instead). By driving cattle north to Kansas, they could sell them for $25 or $30 a head, maybe more. It was an opportunity that many Texans took advantage of for as long as they could.

THE FIRST CATTLE DRIVES

The era of the cattle drives remained an open window for about a generation, from the mid-1860s until the 1880s. But such drives were not easy.

One of the key originators of the Texas–Kansas cattle drives of the 1860s was a young livestock broker from Illinois, named Joseph G. McCoy. After paying a visit to Topeka, Kansas, McCoy wrote a letter to the governor of Kansas encouraging the importation of Texas longhorns to frontier Kansas railheads and their shipment back East. He then went

A photograph of a cowboy from 1887. His hat kept the sun out of his eyes and the rain off his neck. A cloth bandana protected his neck from the sun and could be pulled over his face to keep out the dust.

to Abilene, Kansas, where he established the system needed to accommodate cattle that had been driven up from Texas. This included a large fenced stockyard, a working barn, an official office, a set of cattle scales, a hotel for drovers and even a bank to handle their money and his. He then dispatched a cattle representative into northern Texas to convince the locals to round up their herds and deliver them to Abilene.

By the end of summer 1867, herds were arriving in the dusty Kansas settlement, now an official "cowtown." By September, 20 railcars were loaded with cows, headed for the stockyards and slaugherhouses of Chicago. Of the 35,000 head of beef that reached Abilene that year, 20,000 wound up in McCoy's stockyards. The era of the cattle drives had opened.

The Cattle Trails

Over the next several years, a handful of working cattle trails developed, including the Chisholm Trail, which forked off to stockyards at either Wichita or Abilene. This trail dated back to before the Civil War, when it was pioneered by a mixed-blood Indian trader named Jesse Chisholm. Estimates suggest that of the millions of cattle herded north out of Texas from the 1860s to the 1880s, approximately half of them were driven along the Chisholm Trail.

A second important cattle route was the Shawnee Trail, which cattlemen used as early as the 1840s. It extended out of south-central Texas, through Dallas, then toward Missouri, where it branched out into sub-routes leading to Kansas City, Sedalia, and St. Louis.

A third route was the Goodnight-Loving Trail, named in 1866 for two trail men, Charles Goodnight and Oliver Loving. This trail also originated in south Texas, but veered across the western part of the state, crossing and recrossing the Pecos River into New Mexico, then turning north through eastern Colorado to Cheyenne, Wyoming, a rail stop along the Union Pacific Railroad that was later completed in 1869. This trail brought beef on the hoof to western mining camps, as well as ranches in Colorado and Wyoming.

CATTLE TRAILS AND RAILHEADS

A map of the major cattle trails shows they ran north from Texas to the cow towns and railroads crossing the Great Plains. Mostly they followed trails first used by Native Americans, traders, and settlers. Between 1865 and 1890 about 10 million cattle were led along the trails.

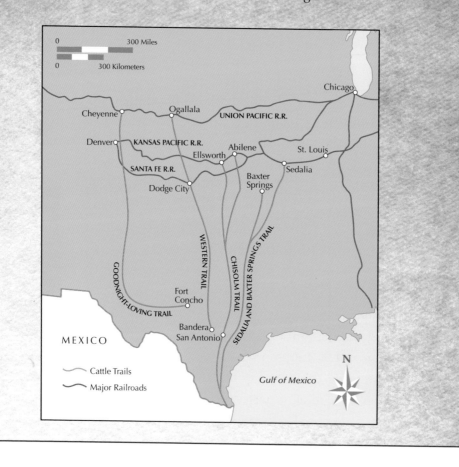

The fourth cattle route was the Western Trail, established later, during the 1870s. This route followed a straight northerly direction across central Oklahoma to Dodge City. There the cattle could be sold and shipped out on the Atchison, Topeka & Santa Fe Railroad.

A COWBOY'S WORK

Regardless of which trail a group of cattle drovers chose to move their herd along, the work was brutal, dirty, and low paying. To begin with, they were driving longhorns, some of the toughest, meanest animals on four hooves. Perhaps the only advantage represented by the longhorn was its trail worthiness. Charles Goodnight observed this attribute, again, as Dykstra notes:

> *Their hoofs are superior to those of any other cattle. In stampedes, they hold together better, are easier circled in a run, and rarely split off when you commence to turn the front. No animal of the cow kind will shift and take care of itself under all conditions as will the Longhorns. They can go farther without water and endure more suffering than others.*

The mathematics of the typical trail drive were simple. It required between 10 and 15 cowboys, including a trail boss and a camp cook, accompanied by a herd of 10 times as many horses. They would drive approximately 2,000 head of three-year-old steers over a rugged western route for a minimum of several hundred miles. According to Texas rancher Charley Goodnight, the average steer needed 30 gallons (135 l) of water a day and access to 10 acres (4 hectares) of good grass, or twice that area if the grass was dry and poor. On average, one cowboy was responsible for 250 to 400 head of cattle, although everyone was ultimately responsible for the entire herd.

The cowboy's work was not for the timid. They were constantly exposed to the weather, which, at its harshest, included everything from a scorching sun to thunderstorms accompanied by hail. The food was usually poor and often monotonous. Those cowhands who rode behind the herd, a position called "riding drag," usually had the worst end of things, as the dust kicked up by thousands of longhorns filtered into their noses and eyes. One cowboy, as noted by historian Hine, "remembered the dust, thick as fur, on the eyebrows of the drag men, and the black phlegm they coughed up for weeks after the drive." Much of their labor had a similar rhythm to it—riding slowly along with a loping herd of cattle amid dust, sometimes mud, and manure. But there were moments when the tedium was punctuated by excitement, as when a herd stampeded or when a violent storm swept over the herd, threatening both man and beast.

MEN OF THE TRAIL

The men who drove cattle from Texas along the various western trails were a mixed group, representing a variety of races and ethnic groups. Most were white, often young men who had grown up in the West. Significant numbers were black, Mexican, or American Indian. Some historians suggest that approximately one out of every three cowboys was nonwhite. Among those from Louisiana or southeast Texas, one in four were black. One black cowboy, a former slave named Bose Ikard, rode with Goodnight and Loving and worked on Goodnight's JA Ranch. One of the West's most famous black cowboys was Nate Love, who later wrote a book about his western exploits. Indians were commonplace, especially from the Cherokee people, who lived in modern-day Oklahoma. One western cattleman, according to historian Hine, suggested that Indian cowboys were "the best in the world." Mexican cowboys were always in demand, as they often had

A photograph from about 1890 of cowboys driving cattle in Wyoming. To catch a runaway animal, the cowboy would usually swing the noose of his rope, the lariat, over his head and try to throw it over the animal's head or horns.

the most experience with handling cattle and were most familiar with the techniques needed, including roping.

In command of the typical cattle drive was the trail boss, a man of special skills and leadership, who often had made the initial investment in the herd and stood to make the most profit from a successful drive. Sometimes, the trail boss was merely hired to lead the drive by the true investor, with the boss receiving three or four times the pay of his cowboys. It was the trail boss who kept his men in line and made certain that things went as smoothly as possible. The boss usually woke up the drive's cook, often the oldest man in the party, to make breakfast and coffee for the men, with the morning meal taking place before sunrise, even as early as 3 or 4 A.M. Before sunrise, cowboys known as "pointers" moved to the head of the herd of cattle. Behind them and running along-side the herd were the swing men, followed by flank riders, then the unfortunates who came up behind the herd, the drag men.

On the Move

Moving the cattle herd along was based on keeping them in a manageable pack, but not so close that they were con-stantly jostling one another. The herd would move at a slow pace, one designed to keep the animals calm, allowing them to stop frequently and graze. As a habit, the cattle positioned themselves in the herd on day one of a drive and usually kept to those places. The animals that took positions at the front of the herd were called "lead steers," and they ultimately led the other animals straight to the loading pen at the end of the trail. Sometimes a lead steer was so reliant that he was taken back to Texas to lead another herd. If calves were born on the trail, cowboys usually slaughtered them, since they could not keep up with the movement of the herd. The same was true of weak or diseased steers.

No matter who they were, the typical cowboy worked hard for little pay. They often earned between $25 and $30 a month—a sum equal to less than $1,000 today. On many cattle drives, alcohol was not allowed, and some bosses even banned profanity.

DANGERS OF THE DRIVE

Most cattle drives from Texas to Kansas took about two months. During this period, anything could happen. The first few days on the trail with a herd were usually the most difficult, as a new herd was more easily spooked and more likely to stampede. The further down the trail the cattle were driven, the better. Cattleman Goodnight once observed, as historian Hine notes, "After a month or two the cattle became gentler."

But stampedes were still unpreventable, unpredictable, and sudden, as described by one cowboy in Hine's book, *The Frontier*:

> *While I was looking at him, this steer leaped into the air, hit the ground with a heavy thud, and gave a grunt that sounded like that of a hog. That was the signal. The whole herd was up and going—and heading right for me. My horse gave a lunge, jerked loose from me, and was away. I barely had time to climb into an oak. The cattle went by like a hurricane, hitting the tree with their horns. It took us all night to round them up. When we got them quieted next morning, we found ourselves six miles from camp.*

Such disruptions were sometimes so common that a single herd might stampede a dozen times in a single night.

Cattle herds were also susceptible to Indian attack. One party of Cheyenne warriors drove off an entire herd in 1870, resulting in a loss of nearly $18,000 for the herd's owner.

Sometimes Indians were more subtle, sneaking up to a herd at night, stealing several cattle, then returning them the following day, as if they had found them loose, to receive a cash reward for their "help." Sometimes a trail boss would cut out a few head of cattle and give them to a group of local Indians, just to keep them from taking cattle on their own. In

This painting by Charles Russell from 1909 is entitled *In Without Knocking*. Cowboys were not allowed to carry guns on the trail but when they were traveling to a cow town they took them in case of trouble. Here the cowboys are riding into a saloon.

other cases of manipulating the situation, an Indian nation might simply charge a per head toll to the trail boss, say a dime a head, which paid for permission to cross Indian land with thousands of cows.

End of the Trail

At the end of the cattle drive, the cattle drovers delivered the herd to the local cattle pens and the trail boss soon sat down with the local livestock buyers to make the sale. Since the cowboys had not likely seen a town in months, and they had just been paid their wages, many of them took the opportunity to sleep in a soft bed, take a real bath and get a real shave, visit the saloon, or the local bawdy house. Many had little to show for their months of work after a few days letting off steam in a cow town. As one old cattle drover remembered years later, notes historian R. R. Dykstra: "Like most of the boys of the early days, I had to sow my wild oats, and I regret to say that I also sowed all of the money I made right along with the oats."

CATTLE AS BIG BUSINESS

In time, those who engaged in the cattle business came to see the cattle drive as an unnecessary leg in the process of making money from Texas cattle. In 1884, meeting in Dodge City, the Western Kansas Cattle Growers' Association called for the end of the annual summer cattle drives from Texas. They might not have even bothered, for, by that time, only a small number of drives were still being made. By 1885 almost 7 million head of cattle had been driven out of Texas, leaving local herds of longhorns largely depleted. Then there were the longhorns themselves, which had never represented a choice cattle breed, as lean and mealy-nosed as they were.

By the 1880s ranching was replacing the cattle drives. Easterners and even foreign investors had made note of the

THE COWBOY LEGEND

Through countless movies, television shows, and books, perhaps no one is more legendary than the American cowboy of the late nineteenth century. He has been constantly portrayed (even as he was in his own time through dime novels and Wild West shows) as a rugged, no nonsense individualist—hard riding, hard drinking, a man ready with his fists, and armed with a six-shooter that he was willing to draw at the slightest provocation. Along with his reputation came the reputations of the Kansas cow towns he frequented, places known for their saloons, gambling tables, and prostitutes.

Not every part of the cowboy legend appears to have been entirely true. One of the most colorful aspects of a cowboy's life was his tendency to rely on his handgun, causing the deaths of anyone who got in his way. This was rarely the case. In Dodge City, for example, only five murders occurred during its ten seasons as a railhead for cattle drives. Dodge, it seems, actually saw more murders before its cattle days, when, during one earlier year, the city was the site of 15 murders. Between Dodge City, Abilene, Wichita, and Caldwell combined, only two murders on average took place during each cattle drive season. Considering that cow towns provided opportunities to combine young cowboys together with guns and alcohol, one might have expected more murders.

How firearms were used by cowboys in cow towns also differs from the popular image. Often, cowboys have been portrayed facing off in dusty western streets, engaging in a "high-noon" shootout. In reality it appears that such face-offs rarely happened at all. Handguns did kill people in these western towns, but fewer than one out of three of the victims died in a mutual exchange of gunfire. Many were unarmed, shot down by someone with a handgun. Most cowboys were not particularly skilled with their handguns and many such guns were not that accurate, even at close range. On top of all this, many western handgun victims actually accidentally shot themselves while taking off their clothes, or by jamming their guns into their trousers.

profits generated even from rounding up a raw herd in one state and driving them overland to another to get them to market. But what if the cattle could simply be raised closer to already existing railroad lines, which could eliminate the drive altogether? This was to become the future of the western cattle industry.

Investments soon poured into western ranching. The government purchased 50,000 head of cattle annually by the early 1880s, largely to provide meat allotments to western Indians living on reservations. In 1881 more than 100 million pounds (45 million kilograms) of beef were exported just to Britain. Such ranches were carefully managed and developed as cattle operations where beefier breeds were raised. Selective breeding soon became the norm. Cowboys were still employed to work the herds, but the days of the cattle drive became a memory.

Wiped Out but Not Forgotten

Western ranching had its own problems, however. Ranches often had to compete with the great influx of farmers for available land and water resources. Some farmers strung up fences of barbed wire, invented in 1867 and designed to keep cattle from roaming on their property. Also, ranches competed with one another for grazing land. By the mid-1880s ranches found themselves holding a glut of cattle and the value of beef began to drop significantly, driving some ranchers out of business.

Then, beginning in the summer of 1886, a weather pattern hit the Great Plains with a long dry spell that left streams, lakes, and other water sources dried up. Summer was followed by the harsh winter of 1886–1887, the worst on record to that date. Blizzards hit the free-ranging herds hard, with some trying to move beyond the storms to safety, only to be stopped by barbed-wire fences, leaving them no place to go. Across the northern plains, cattle ranches experienced losses of up to 90 percent of their animals.

The year 1887 marked an end to the heyday of the cattle industry across the West, just over 20 years since the first cattle drives had hit the trails out of Texas. While ranching continued, profits were never as high as they had been during the heyday of the 1860s, 1870s, and early 1880s. Ranchers were forced to adopt new methods of ranching and handling their herds. Costs continued to rise, yet beef prices remained low. Nevertheless, the days of the cattle drives, of the independent-minded cowboy, and of cattle as an important and profitable natural resource of the West never fully ended, leaving their mark on the West of the nineteenth century and beyond.

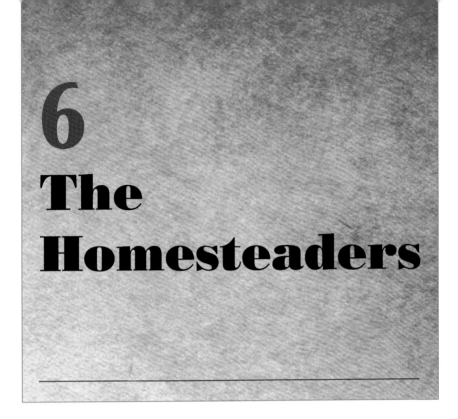

6
The
Homesteaders

During the nearly three generations following the purchase of the Louisiana Territory— lands that included the vast stretches of the Great Plains—from the French in 1803, Americans avoided trying their hand at farming these daunting grasslands. Even as late as 1860, on the eve of the Civil War, the general line of settlement extended from St.Paul, Minnesota, to Fort Worth, Texas, then southward on to the banks of the Rio Grande. Only a hearty few had ventured out to eastern Kansas and Nebraska by the 1850s, and to southeastern Dakota by 1860. Nearly every acre of land between Texas and Canada was still wilderness, home to Indians and buffalo.

THE "GREAT AMERICAN DESERT"
It is understandable why farmers and their families avoided the Great Plains for farming. For one, there was still plenty of land available elsewhere: good, rich soil in the tier of states

hugging the western Mississippi River, including Iowa, Minnesota, Missouri, Arkansas, and eastern Texas. Why would any reasonably thinking farmer pack up his family and possessions and move them to a place like western Kansas, land that had been described for decades as part of the "Great American Desert"? U.S. Army Major Stephen Long had given the Great Plains that label following his exploration of the region in 1819–20. Writing his official report, Long had called the plains the "haunt of bison and jackal," and added: "I do not hesitate in giving the opinion, that it is almost wholly uninhabitable by a people depending upon agriculture for their subsistence." Historian G. C. Fite notes how, even 40 years later, General William Tecumseh Sherman, writing while in northeastern Colorado, declared "the government will have to pay a bounty for people to live up here till necessity forces them."

Yet others writing during the 1860s were beginning to express views supporting farming on the Great Plains. The curve leading to this change of view had been about a generation in coming. Since the founding of the American republic, the U.S. government had made a practice of selling land lying further and further west. The Land Ordinance of 1785 had set the price for 640 acres (260 ha) of land—equal to a square mile of property—at $1 an acre. Many farmers could not rustle up $640 to purchase land, so the law helped land speculators and eastern capitalists. Through the early decades of the nineteenth century, additional land laws were passed, reducing the number of acres farmers were required to purchase from the government down to only 40 (16 ha), while even allowing purchasers to buy on credit.

LAND LEGISLATION

By the 1840s some American citizens were encouraging the government to provide free western land to farmers. In 1841

Congress passed the Log Cabin Bill, which allowed Americans living on the remote frontier to occupy land without legal title, at least until civilization caught up with them. Still the call for free land from the government became louder and louder. A labor leader in New York, George Henry Evans, suggested a government plan to offer 160 acres (65 ha) of western farmland to anyone willing to move to it and make suitable improvements. He had his reasons. With too many people living in America's Eastern cities, largely due to large numbers of European immigrants, there were not enough jobs and workers' wages were kept low. Opening up the West with the offer of free land would, wrote Evans, as historian Robert Hine notes: "carry off the superabundant labor [of Eastern cities] to the . . . fertile West."

Evans's idea of free public land in the West had its own supporters, including the influential editor of the *New York Weekly Tribune,* Horace Greeley. He believed that occupying the West would prove to be good for business in New York, as western farmers would rely on Eastern merchants and manufacturing for their farming operations. Greeley also believed in the need for a western "safety valve," to relieve the crowding of cities in the East. For several years Greeley kept up the drum beat of support for a program of free government land, and his writings were symbolized by the words he later became famous for: "Go West, young man."

In the 1850s the newly formed Republican Party gave its hearty support to a homestead plan, largely in an attempt to extend its political influence as a fledgling party across the West. But legislation was blocked in Congress by Southerners, who feared that the settlers who moved onto the Great Plains would largely come from the North and, thus, spread the doctrine of anti-slavery into any new western territories. When the territory of Kansas was formed in 1854, that very fear ripped the region apart through the violence that became known as "Bleeding Kansas." So another decade passed without a congressional act to provide free land on the plains.

ONE HUNDRED AND SIXTY ACRES

In the early 1860s other national events cleared the way for homestead legislation. Southern objections no longer mattered, as the Southern states left the Union to form the Confederacy in 1861. Against the backdrop of the Civil War, Congress passed, in 1862, the "Act to Secure Homesteads to Actual Settlers on the Public Domain." It was a complicated title for a fairly simple piece of legislation.

Taking effect on January 1, 1863, the Homestead Act made available to individuals over the age of 21—both men and women, U.S. citizens and foreign-born immigrants— 160 acres (65 ha) of western land by simply filing the appropriate fees, costing around $10. All that was required of any would-be homesteader was to make "improvements" on the land, such as putting it under the plow and building a house or outbuildings, such as a barn, and to live on their chosen claim for a total of five years. At that time, the terms of the "deal" between the federal government and the homesteader were met, and the land became his or hers, free and clear. Decades of talk about free land in the West had finally become reality.

The Homestead Act was met with anxious excitement by hundreds of thousands of Americans and immigrants and their families. All told, 400,000 families made claims on 285 million acres (115 million ha) of land, an exchange of land from the government to private citizens on a massive scale. Yet the impact of the Homestead Act needs to be placed in perspective. During the 70 years leading up to the passage of the act, approximately 700 million acres (283 million ha) of public land had become privately owned, with people buying land from the government, not receiving it free. So for every 160 acres (65 ha) of land on the frontier claimed under the Homestead Act, another 400 acres (160 ha) were bought and paid for. This means that the majority of western lands claimed by settlers were not gained freely through the Homestead Act, but bought, much of it through the Log Cabin Bill.

Homesteaders in Minnesota as pictured in a photograph, painted over in oils, from about 1870. Grandparents, parents, and children lived together on the homestead.

NOT ALL LAND FOR THE TAKING

However, there were restrictions placed on what lands could be claimed under the Homestead legislation of 1862. Homesteaders could only claim land that had first been surveyed. (Under the Log Cabin Bill, settlers could claim unsurveyed federal land as squatters, then purchase it later, after a survey had been completed and the appropriate papers could be drawn up.) Also, homesteaders were not allowed to stake claims on land taken from American Indians in the West, territory equal to approximately 100 million acres (40 million ha) following 1862.

Since western surveying progressed slowly, many acres remained unavailable to would-be homesteaders. An additional 140 million acres (56 million ha) of western land was unavailable under the act, as it was ceded to the states to be sold to fund "land-grant colleges." The federal property granted to the advancing railroad lines across the West was also exempt, a checkerboard of lands held by the railways in alternating sections, paralleling the steel ribbons of rail. Even though Great Plains farmers would need close access to railroads, this put another 183 million acres (74 million ha) out of reach.

Such lands—land grant college acreages, railroad properties, former Indian territories, and all unsurveyed property—were thus eliminated as options for the prospective homesteader. These federal or formerly federal lands might be available for purchase, but that was no different a situation than farmers had always had. Since some of these lands were choice properties in the West, homesteaders were often left with properties that were less than ideal in location.

BYPASSING THE LAW

Still, thousands upon thousands of homestead claims were filed. The first was made on January 1, 1863—the very day the Homestead Act went into effect—on a claim near Beatrice, Nebraska. Yet the real momentum for filing homestead claims did not kick in until the late 1860s and early 1870s. In 1871 alone, 20,000 people filed claims on 2.5 million acres (1 million ha) of land along the Minnesota–Dakota border, as well as along the Nebraska–Kansas frontier. In 1871 and 1872, 9,000 claims were filed each year for land in Kansas alone. More claims came in subsequent years. Kansas saw 43,000 homestead claims between 1885 and 1887, while the Dakota Territory witnessed 22,000 filed claims.

While significant numbers of applicants filed their claims legitimately, intending to abide by both the spirit and the letter of the free land law, others did not. The Homestead Act was a partial failure due to people using unscrupulous methods to get around the conditions and gain property unethically. While Congress had ideally set up a system to put free land in the hands of small-scale farmers, significant amounts of land were accumulated by powerful ranchers, mining companies, and others.

One method of getting around the intent of the law was in the area of making "improvements" on the property. People sometimes built little, hand-held models of cabins or other buildings and placed them on a claim so that a witness could testify that he had seen a building on the property in question. Alternatively, a 6-foot (1.8-m) square cabin would be constructed on a wagon bed and moved from claim to claim, for the same purpose.

Land speculation companies sometimes hired men to take out homestead claims, then sign over their land rights to the company. The same practice was carried out by cattle ranchers' hired hands and lumber company employees, allowing the rancher or the lumber company owner to accumulate thousands of acres of connected land claims as their own. In a notorious case, one lumber mill, the California Redwood

Company in San Francisco, took sailors from foreign ships tied up in the harbor to the local courthouse, where they helped their recruits to file citizenship papers. They then took them to the local land office to file timber claims, then off to a lawyer or notary to witness the sailors signing over their claim to the lumber company. Each sailor was paid $50 for his cooperation.

THE TRIALS OF HOMESTEADING

While some who filed homestead claims cheated their way to landownership, there were many who came to the Great Plains simply looking to start a new life. Even though U.S. Department of Agriculture officials suggested that all homesteaders needed approximately $1,000 to start up their western farming ventures—to cover the costs of equipment, seed, fences, livestock, and moving—many who moved out West came with less. Many were poor and drawn by the offer of free land. Endless thousands came from the East, both from Northern and Southern states. Once slavery was ended during the Civil War, many former black slaves moved to homesteads in Oklahoma and Kansas as "Exodusters," intent on putting down roots in a new environment. Hundreds of thousands of homesteaders weren't Americans at all, but were Germans, Swedes, Czechs, Norwegians, and other immigrants. By 1900 one out of every three non-Indian residents of Texas was a German immigrant. So many Europeans moved out to the Great Plains that, despite large numbers who settled in Eastern cities, by 1900 the plains boasted the highest percentage of foreign-born residents.

Since the Homestead Act did not discriminate against women—female homestead applicants merely had to be 21 years old and unmarried—the act drew many women out onto the plains. Through the early decades of the Homestead Act to the end of the century, women in some regions of the plains constituted between 5 and 15 percent of homestead claims. After 1900 the percentage rose to around 20 percent. Historians estimate that between 30,000 and 40,000 claims were made by women who filed in their own names. Of those tens of thousands of intrepid female homesteaders, the success rate was about the same as for men who filed claims.

A High Failure Rate

Yet even for those who filed legitimate claims, moved to their land, and tried to make a go of farming and building a life, the failure rate was high, amounting to around half of all homesteaders. Buying everything needed to farm the western lands was expensive and, if good crops were not produced during the first harvest or two, a homestead family could be broke. Just moving one's family to some of these distant claims was expensive. For a family of five, railroad tickets alone might cost the equivalent of half a year's income. Some found their remote homesteads so isolated that they could not stand the lack of human contact. Others farmed on claims too far from a railroad to get their farm products to market.

So many things could and did go wrong for those trying to make their living on homesteads in Kansas, Nebraska, and elsewhere that failing was as common as success. Thus, in western Kansas and Nebraska, between 1888 and 1892, half of all homesteaders failed, many moving somewhere back East. Historian Jon E. Lewis recalls one failed homesteader, who left a note behind at his abandoned prairie house: "250 miles to the nearest post office; 100 miles to wood; 20 miles to water; 6 inches to hell. Gone to live with the wife's folks."

POPULATING THE GREAT PLAINS

Even though the Homestead Act was not as successful as Congress had planned, the latter decades of the nineteenth

Great Plains Soddies

One of the many challenges that homesteaders on the Great Plains faced was the lack of building materials for their houses. On the northern plains, tree growth was limited to riverbanks. Since most of these trees were soft cottonwoods, the would-be plains farmer had to adjust his thinking away from using wood to build his house to something much less glamorous—prairie sod.

Sod houses came to dot the Great Plains across Kansas, Nebraska, and beyond. Using a "grasshopper plow," which was pulled by a team of horses or oxen, farmers cut the tough prairie ground into blocks of earth, sometimes called "Nebraska marble." Such blocks usually measured about 1 foot (30 centimeters) across and 3 feet (1 m) in length. Farm families then placed them side by side, creating earthen walls 3 feet (1 m) thick, which their occupants discovered provided significant insulation against the bitter winters of the Great Plains.

A typical sod house, or "soddy," measured approximately 18 by 24 feet (5 by 7 m) and could be built in about a week. The necessary wood for a door, windows, and support timbers could be bought in a nearby town, or through a mail order catalog. A pair of forked tree trunks might be erected to support the ridgepole. Rough rafters were added, covered over with tar paper (if the owner could afford it), and a layer of sod bricks placed on top to make the roof. By summer, the roof would be covered in grass. Such a simple building was cheap to construct, maybe costing less than $10. As historian Jon Lewis notes, a soddy was "warm in winter, cool in summer, bullet-proof, fireproof, and would last for a decade or more." Such houses were still in use in some parts of Nebraska and Kansas as late as the 1930s.

These dirt houses did have their problems. They were dark inside, and the earth gave off a constant dank smell. Then there was the smell of dried buffalo dung used as fuel. "Buffalo chips" were burned in the stove to provide energy for cooking and heating. Added to this, insects and snakes often lived in the walls.

The story is told of a homesteading family who laid down to sleep, only to have one of the two young boys complaining of being pinched by his brother, who denied being guilty. The parents instructed the boys to get quiet and go to sleep. The following morning, the alleged "pinches" were explained. The boy lay dead in his bed, victim of a rattlesnake bite, the snake having disappeared into the sod walls.

1. Stable
2. Wagon
3. Plow
4. Grass sod roof
5. Earth sod wall
6. Buffalo dung fuel
7. Washing clothes
8. Main room
9. Stove
10. Bedroom
11. Outside privy
12. Kitchen garden

A homesteader's settlement with the main sod house cut away to show details of the main room.

century witnessed a tidal wave of migration out onto the Great Plains specifically, and across the West generally. Americans moving West settled more farmland between 1865 and the turn of the century than during the previous 250 years. Much of this settlement took place on the prairies and plains of Minnesota, Iowa, eastern Nebraska, and Kansas. Across these lands, the annual rainfall was normally adequate to support farming, as Easterners tried to replicate their traditional "corn and hog" farms further West.

Dividing Lines

Generally, the line separating farmable from unfarmable land was the 100th Meridian, the line of north-south latitude that divided the Dakotas and Nebraska in half and separated the western third of Kansas from its eastern portions. Generally, east of this line, the average annual rainfall was between 20 and 40 inches (500 and 1,000 millimeters)—enough for sustainable agriculture. But west of the 100th Meridian, the rainfall averaged half that amount, from 10 to 20 inches (250 to 500 mm). In this region the rolling waves of prairie grass surrendered to Great Plains ground cover that included bluestem and buffalo grass, which were tough on the plow and almost indestructible.

With much of the Great Plains representing a geographic challenge to nineteenth-century farmers, those who moved out into the country's Midwest typically had to change their lives dramatically. Families who had lived back East in a log cabin or even a clapboard house might have to build their new house on the plains out of chunks of sod, since in many places there were not enough trees to cut into a shelter. They burned dried dung, called buffalo chips, which lay scattered across the region. If a homestead was established at a distance from a local stream or river, farmers had to sink wells down hundreds of feet, relying on newfangled drilling equipment. To pull the water out of the ground, windmills were set up. Soon, the plains were dotted with store-bought, steel-bladed, platform mills.

THE CHALLENGE OF WEATHER

Some farmers managed to time the establishment of their homesteads just right for the weather. During the late 1870s through the mid-1880s, the Great Plains experienced a wet cycle, with more rain falling than usual. With such rains came an influx of homesteaders into the remote reaches of the plains, including western Texas, western Kansas and Nebraska, and other normally dry regions. One Nebraska land developer, Charles Dana Wilbur, even imagined in 1881 that farmers themselves might have caused the change in weather pattern, claiming that, as noted by historian Robert Hine: "Rain follows the plow."

But many of those who took a chance on moving onto the usually drier parts of the Great Plains received a rude wake up call in 1886, when the rains dried up, bringing a drought that continued until the mid-1890s. It was as if nature had played a cruel trick on the homesteaders who had put down roots on the plains during the previous decade or so. As the novelist Stephen Crane wrote, according to Hine: "The farmers [were] helpless, with no weapon against this terrible and inscrutable wrath of nature. The country died." The result was that many homesteaders could not produce an adequate crop or maintain enough livestock, and were forced to surrender their claims.

Overcoming the Difficulties

The drought did not last forever, though, and a fresh wave of homesteaders moved onto the Great Plains when a new wet cycle began after 1896. This, and other factors, gave rise to another land rush into the West. Between 1900 and

1909, another wave of thousands of Americans and newly arrived immigrants established their homes in the western Dakotas and eastern Montana. Survival for this generation of "sod busters" was eased by new innovations, including the introduction of tough, drought resistant grains such as "Turkey Red" wheat (also known as durum wheat), an Asian import variety. Farmers had also learned to "dry farm," which included deeper plowing to help the ground retain moisture, as well as harrowing the surface of fields to protect them with a natural "dry mulch," to keep evaporation to a minimum. Such techniques helped, but did not insure crops against a drought cycle that kicked in again in 1910.

A FIELD OF INNOVATION

Aiding the western farmers of the late nineteenth century, as well as farmers in others parts of the United States, were the innovative changes in farming equipment. Following the Civil War, American farming witnessed a series of technological advances, all designed to ease the plight of farmers and to increase their productivity.

Something as simple as the plowshare changed significantly, with the switch from iron to steel blades. A farmer's time preparing his fields for sowing a crop was cut down by the introduction of "gang plows," which allowed for several rows to be plowed at the same time, rather than just one. Mechanized reaping machines were introduced, that, according to historian Robert Hine, "mowed, raked, and loaded hay and made it possible to load a ton of hay from a field in just five minutes." New machines were invented, one right after the other, each making its own contribution to western farming—self-raking reapers, automatic binders, power threshers, with later models powered by coal-burning steam boilers. By 1880 the first "combine" was at work in American fields, a machine that "combined" harvesting and threshing together. Within just a few years, huge steam-powered combines were in use, capable of producing 1,800 sacks of grain in a single day.

BONANZA FARMS

With the introduction of a higher level of mechanization to farming on the Great Plains, a new type of "corporate" farm came into existence. Known as "bonanza farms," these large-scale farming businesses dotted great expanses of the northern plains and the fertile valley of central California. Such operations were typically owned by a corporation, and covered thousands of acres. One of the largest was a farm that covered 34,000 acres (14,000 ha) outside of Fargo, North Dakota, operated by Oliver Dalrymple. His wheat fields stretched across 13,000 endless acres (5,200 ha). A bonanza operation would employ teams of farmers, each working their own corner of the farm, with some groups of workers never seeing others for an entire farming season. Out in California, bonanza farms were set up on thousands of acres, the land often sold off by the Central Pacific Railroad. One such farm covered 66,000 acres (27,000 ha) of land, where a beehive of hundreds of employees managed to produce one million bushels of farm produce a year. As early as 1880, California, in part due to its bonanza operations, was the greatest wheat producing state in the Union.

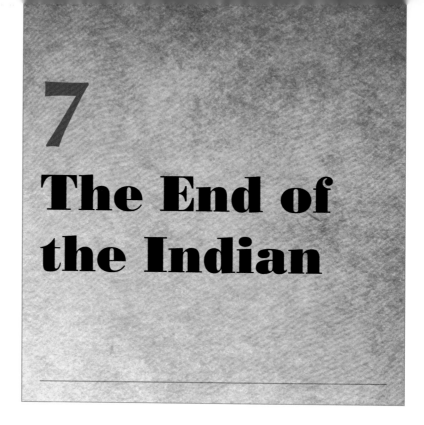

7

The End of the Indian

During the decades following the Civil War, American Indians in the West nearly became an endangered species. Throughout the previous 250 years, Europeans had dominated the Western Hemisphere, carrying out national policies that varied from trying to convert Native Americans to Christianity to working to annihilate them. In the latter years of the eighteenth and early nineteenth centuries, the government of the United States tried two alternate policies for dealing with Indians: assimilation and displacement. Assimilation involved trying to convince Native Americans to accept Anglo-American culture, while displacement meant removing them from lands east of the Mississippi River and sending them to the Great Plains. In the 1830s dozens of Eastern Indian nations were removed by congressional act to a strip of land on the plains, which extended north from modern-day Oklahoma to eastern Kansas and Nebraska.

By 1865 few native culture groups remained in the path of Americans moving farther west; at least, to the edges of the Trans-Mississippi West. But, over the following generation to 1890, the last great Indian "barrier" to the westward migration of Anglo-Americans was to be removed. The causes of that removal included constant government pressure on the Indians to accept less land for themselves, the near elimination of the Great Plains buffalo herds, and the power of the American military.

AN ERA OF RAIDING

Indian and non-Indian conflicts in the Trans-Mississippi West were nothing new in 1865. As early as the 1820s and 1830s Indians in the West were attacking American fur trappers and mountain men. The Kiowa and Comanche swooped down on wagon trains passing along the Santa Fe Trail during the 1830s. The California Gold Rush had caused whites and Indians to fight one another over land during the late 1840s and early 1850s. In 1854 conflicts arose between soldiers garrisoned at modern-day Wyoming's Fort Laramie and Lakota (Sioux) Indians. During the late 1850s and early 1860s, Comanches on the Southern Plains and Paiute Indians in today's Nevada fought soldiers, western emigrants, and even Pony Express riders. In 1862 the Santee Lakota in Minnesota turned to the warpath, killing whites for weeks on end, and nearly causing the territory to be abandoned by non-Indians.

Such attacks were often brought on when western Indian groups felt pressured by an encroaching white presence, or taken advantage of, for example by signing a treaty with the government, only to have whites continue occupying their land. For many whites, Indians only posed a problem. They stood in the way of American "progress," the advance of Americans across the continent. When Indians "went on the warpath," westerners thought only two responses were plausible. First, that the army should intervene to protect them and remove the Indians to reservations, where they could be watched closely. The second choice was less considered, but still suggested: To exterminate them, simply kill off an entire Indian nation so its members would not ever prove a threat again. Perhaps one of the most infamous examples of the second response was the Sand Creek Massacre, which took place in November 1864.

SHAME AT SAND CREEK

During the previous summer Northern Cheyenne and Arapaho warriors had attacked several settlers in western Kansas and eastern Colorado, after various white groups had occupied lands granted to the Indians under the Fort Laramie Treaty of 1851. In September tribal leaders were invited to a peace conference at Fort Weld near Denver, where several chiefs agreed to stop fighting. In exchange, government officials promised to protect them from civilian militia groups if they camped near Fort Lyon, a local army post. But, by October, the Indians who showed up at Fort Lyon were told by the post's commander, Major Scott Anthony, that the army could no longer feed them and that they must leave. Cheyenne Chief Black Kettle and Arapaho leader Left Hand soon led 700 of their people to a site 40 miles (65 km) away along Sand Creek. With winter coming on, another 600 Arapaho moved further east along the Arkansas River.

In telling the Cheyenne and Arapaho to move on, Major Anthony was working together with Colorado's territorial Governor, John Evans, and a minister-turned-militia officer, Colonel John M. Chivington—two men intent on removing Indians from their territory. In late November Chivington led 700 volunteer militia in an attack against the Indians encamped along Sand Creek. He gave orders to spare no one, even the women and children. As a result the white militiamen killed more than 150 Indians, with two out of three being women, children, or old men. Only nine of Chivington's men were killed. All of Denver lauded the militia attack, calling the men heroes. Chivington even appeared during an evening performance at the Denver opera house, where he displayed 100 Cheyenne scalps, with those in attendance leaping to their feet and applauding.

Fortunately, Chivington did not remain on a hero's pedestal for long. Regular U.S. Army officers saw the Colorado minister's attack as an unprovoked massacre. Back East General Ulysses S. Grant referred to the militia's actions as nothing less than murder. Investigations were held by Congress and the army, and Chivington was disgraced, forced to surrender his militia rank and uniform. But news of the attack against innocent and peaceful Indian women and children spread quickly, reaching northern bands of the Cheyenne, Arapaho, and Lakota. Suddenly, whites across the West were targets of Indian attack. This included stagecoaches, remote settlers, and even whole towns. Julesburg, Colorado, was attacked by Cheyenne, who sacked the frontier community. Across the southern plains, the Kiowa and Comanche carried out multiple raids.

INDIANS AT ARMS

One of the Great Plains nations most stirred by the Sand Creek Massacre was the Teton Sioux. They had already been at odds with other whites in recent years. Among those who led the way in fighting against white encroachment onto Lakota land was Red Cloud. His campaign against the army to drive whites out of the Powder River region was a textbook effort that continued year after year during the 1860s.

After five years of fighting, Red Cloud and his followers had managed to cut off almost all western traffic along

The 7th U.S. Cavalry under Lieutenant Colonel George Custer attack Black Kettle's Cheyenne village at Washita River, Oklahoma, on November 23, 1868. The action was taken in revenge for Indian attacks on ranches, stagecoaches, and wagon trains that had resulted in the murder of more than 150 Americans.

the Bozeman Trail. In the spring of 1868 the commander of the Military Division of the Missouri, General William Tecumseh Sherman, called a peace council, again at Fort Laramie. The peace commissioners came ready to give up the military posts along the Powder River near the Bozeman Trail to make peace with the Sioux. Red Cloud was hesitant to cooperate, ready to wait until the forts were already given up, before he would sit down and talk. As historian Allen Weinstein notes, Red Cloud said: "When we see the soldiers moving away and the forts abandoned, then I will come down and talk." The army had no choice but to give up their western posts. On July 29, 1868, Fort C. F. Smith was evacuated and the following day, Red Cloud's warriors burned it to the ground. The next month Fort Phil Kearny was left, with the Northern Cheyenne subsequently razing it. The last of the posts, Fort Reno, was given up just days later, and Red Cloud emerged the victor. The Bozeman Trail was no longer a western thoroughfare for whites.

Then Red Cloud lived up to his word and came to Fort Laramie. He arrived on November 6 to talk peace, with the war already over. A new treaty was written up which included the government's promise, notes Weinstein, that "if bad men among the whites . . . shall commit any wrong upon the person or property of the Indians," the government would intervene and arrest the perpetrators. New reservation boundaries were established, new lands set aside for Indian occupation, and additional assurances were made to the negotiating Native Americans.

DESTROYING THE BUFFALO

But only a few days would pass before whites violated the 1868 Fort Laramie Treaty. In a sense, Indians also broke the treaty, but their lapses were, perhaps, a result of misunderstanding. The leaders of the various Indian nations who

Buffalo hunters photographed in Montana in 1882. On horseback and armed with a Sharp's rifle, a skilled hunter could kill more than 100 buffalo before a herd stampeded. In a season he might kill as many as 3,000 buffalo.

signed the treaty thought they still had the right to hunt buffalo, wherever they might roam. The treaty, however, limited them to certain regions to hunt. The larger intent of the government was to encourage the western tribes to stop roaming around, settle down, and ultimately assimilate by becoming farmers on reservation land with government agents close by to monitor their movements.

Another complication that made it difficult for Indians to abide by the limits the treaty placed on them was the destruction of the bison on the Great Plains by non-Indian buffalo hunters. The federal government were encouraging professional buffalo killers to spread out across the Plains and slaughter as many bison as they could. As one U.S. Army officer, Colonel Richard Dodge, urged a buffalo hunter in 1867, according to historian Robert Hine: "Kill every buffalo you can! Every buffalo dead is an Indian gone."

Buffalo hunters carried out their deadly work in short order. Between 1872 and 1874 non-Indian hunters killed off as many as 3 million bison annually, while the hundreds of thousands of Indians killed only 150,000 head. By the mid-1870s the great bison herds of the Plains were nearly non-existent, and, by the early 1880s, their numbers, which might have reached 30 or 40 million a generation earlier, were reduced to fewer than 1,000.

The days of Indian reliance on bison for their food, shelter, and other purposes were gone. Native Americans who had engaged in the "horse and buffalo" culture for several generations, even as they gave up early forms of farming, now found themselves paupers on the Plains. (The timeframe for wiping out the western bison herds corresponded with the movement of cattle up from Texas on the legendary long drives of the 1860s to 1880s. The cattle replaced the buffalo as the primary animal stock of the Plains, their numbers controlled by whites.)

As a result, Native American nations had no choice but to surrender to reservation life, become dependent on doles of food and supplies, and give up their tribal ways. The outcome was harsh for the Indians forced to live by the white man's rules. As notes historian Allen Weinstein, "the agency [reservation] Indians spent most of their time sitting around, drinking whiskey, and feeling sorry for themselves."

TAKING THE "INDIAN" OUT OF INDIAN

By the 1880s the U.S. government had managed to subdue almost every western Indian nation, placing them on reservations scattered across the West. Here the Native Americans were kept under constant supervision and harassed into becoming farmers capable of raising their own food. Everywhere the Indians turned, someone was telling them what to do and how to behave.

In 1870 the U.S. Supreme Court laid some of the groundwork for the subjugation of the Native Americans by ruling that Congress had the power to renounce any previous treaty it had made with an Indian nation. The following year Congress voted in favor of a resolution that officially ended the practice and necessity of negotiating treaties with American Indian groups. It stated that "No Indian nation or tribe within the territory of the United States shall [henceforth] be acknowledged or recognized as an independent nation, tribe, or power with whom the United States may contract by treaty." Additional legislation was passed during the 1880s, which stripped the Indians of their rights to operate under tribal laws or customs. The days of the independent Native American seemed gone forever.

Then, beginning in the 1880s, a new strategy was employed to further eliminate the Indians' identity, culture, and language. Well-meaning whites, many of them Easterners with little direct experience with Indians, took it upon themselves to further the assimilation of the Indians. Already American Indians had been taken from their lands and placed on

Some Indians found the killing of the bison herds and the humiliation of life under the watchful eye of Indian agents unacceptable, and refused to give in. They became "roamers," who tried to live on their own in small bands, stay on the move, hunt what game they could find, and keep themselves independent of white control. Perhaps 20 percent of the Teton Sioux population, by the 1870s, were roamers.

reservations. Now these Easterners—ministers, government officials, social workers, and reformers—who called themselves "Friends of the Indians," set out to remove Indian children from their families. They believed that, if the children could be taught the ways and values of the white man's culture before Indian parents had an opportunity to instill their native ways in them, then a new generation of assimilated Indians would be created.

To accomplish this goal, young Indians—some as young as five years—were taken from their families and shipped back East to special Indian schools. One such institution was the United States Indian Training and Industrial School at Carlisle, Pennsylvania. At the Carlisle School, Indian boys and girls were forbidden to speak their native languages, to perform traditional dances, or to sing tribal religious songs. The boys lost their long hair and had to wear uniforms, while the girls wore Victorian-era dresses and were taught to play the piano. Anything they brought to the school that was part of their traditional heritage—moccasins, headgear, fetishes, medicine bundles—was typically placed by school officials into a fire and burned. Indian boys who arrived at Carlisle with feathers in their hair and beads around their necks were soon shorn and stripped of their past. Boys were required to wear military uniforms and drill outdoors.

Over a 20-year period, beginning in the early 1880s, two dozen Indian schools were in operation, as well as 81 boarding schools, and nearly 150 day schools located on the reservations. Each had the same purpose—to take the "Indian" out of the Indian.

ANOTHER WAR WITH THE SIOUX

Compounding problems between the government, white civilians, and Indians on the plains, especially among the Lakota, was the discovery of gold in the Black Hills of modern-day South Dakota. When earlier rumors of gold had begun to spread, the government sent a military expedition into the Black Hills to prove that no gold was located there. The campaign, led by General George Armstrong Custer, resulted in the unexpected discovery of gold after all.

The Sioux claimed this land and referred to as *Paha Sapa*, sacred hills that represented the heart of the universe for the Lakota. Although the government had set aside the Dakotas as Indian land under a previous treaty, by 1874 prospectors were beginning to flood into the Black Hills region. Red Cloud, disappointed, went to Washington to visit with President Grant. The meeting (Red Cloud's second in the U.S. capital, having been invited to Washington in 1870) did not go well. Grant informed the Oglalla chief of the government's intention to purchase the Black Hills. Red Cloud pleaded for federal officials to call another council at Fort Laramie to discuss the matter with all the important western chiefs. Grant agreed.

Crazy Horse and Sitting Bull

Indian agents from the Bureau of Indian Affairs went out to Fort Laramie in September 1875, expecting Lakota resistance to fall apart. They did not know how angry the Native Americans were and were shocked to find, once they arrived at the Wyoming fort, 20,000 Indians gathered there to display a wall of resistance against the government's desire to purchase the Black Hills. By this time, too, Red Cloud's voice was taking a second seat to a new generation of Lakota warriors, led by the younger Crazy Horse, along with a powerful Hunkpapa medicine man and prophet, named Sitting Bull.

These two wanted no part in negotiating any more treaties with the white government. When negotiations between government agents and the Indian leaders failed, with the natives showing significant hostility, the government men wisely decided swiftly to pack up quietly and return to Washington, D.C.

Having gained little true insight into the Indian frame of mind, the agents suggested to President Grant that he should take a strong position and force the tribes of the northern plains to abide by government policy. Any Indian "roamers" should report into their reservation. It appears that almost no one in Washington thought a better policy might be to have the government live up to its obligations under the Fort Laramie Treaty of 1868, and send the army into the Black Hills to run out the trespassing prospectors. Grant did, however, dispatch the military to subdue the Indians.

LITTLE BIG HORN

Government agents now began plotting against the very western nations that they were, under American law, responsible for. During a meeting at the White House in November 1875 Bureau agents decided to order all roamers back to their respective reservations by January 31, 1876. The deadline date was a trick, of sorts. Even if roaming bands decided to agree to the government's orders, it would be nearly impossible for them to report in by the end of January, since winter weather and snows would make their movement extremely difficult. Either way, the government established choices for the roamers that could only be to the benefit of the government itself. The Indians would either report in or, if they did not, the government would have an "excuse" to send the military after them.

The year 1876, then, brought another full-scale conflict between northern plains native groups and the U.S. Army.

Among those who fought the Lakota, Cheyenne, and their allies was Colonel Custer, who marched his men from Fort Abraham Lincoln in today's North Dakota. He pursued warriors led by Sitting Bull until he and his Seventh Cavalry encountered them at the junction of the Big Horn and Little Horn Rivers, west of Montana's Rosebud Mountains, on the evening of June 24, 1876. There Custer's scouts informed him of the presence of a small contingent of warriors.

Without proper information and foolishly dividing his forces, Custer led his men into a trap when the Seventh attacked the Indians on the following day. With a force of only 265 men, Custer found himself facing approximately 2,000 hostile Native American warriors, including Sitting Bull and Crazy Horse. The 36-year-old Custer and his entire unit were wiped out in less than an hour, in a battle that troops who arrived later called the Little Bighorn, and which Indians referred to as the battle of the Greasy Grass (their name for the same river).

SUBJUGATION OF THE PLAINS INDIANS

The massacre of Custer and the 7th Cavalry, commonly referred to as "Custer's Last Stand," was a short-lived victory for the American Indians on the Great Plains. Many Americans were shocked by Little Bighorn, and supported delivering a sea of soldiers to avenge the deaths of the cavalrymen. With a vengeance, the army tracked down renegade Indian factions with a calculated swiftness. In May 1877 Crazy Horse finally turned himself in at Fort Robinson, Nebraska, and four months later he was dead, stabbed during a scuffle by a guard's bayonet.

During these same years, other fighting took place across the West between army troops and Indians, including the Apache in the Southwest. Their chief, Cochise, had surrendered to the army in 1872, only to have his successor,

Geronimo, continue a guerrilla war against white miners and the U.S. military. The Red River War of 1874–1875 brought Apache bands in alliance with Kiowas and Comanches. The fighting was extremely bloody, but the army subdued most of the combatants by 1875. Geronimo himself, however, continued fighting until 1886, when he finally surrendered.

An encampment of Brule and Oglala Sioux Indians on White Clay Creek, near Pine Ridge, South Dakota. From 1876, the U.S. government forced most of the hostile Sioux onto reservations in the state, where they remained, subdued and oppressed, for decades.

Sometimes, the army even went to war with tribal nations that had been at peace with the United States. When gold was discovered on the lands of the friendly Nez Perce people in 1860, government agents told them to surrender 90 percent of their lands, a total of 6 million acres (2.4 million ha). Some Nez Perce leaders agreed, while others, such as Chief Tukekas, refused. His son, Chief Joseph, led a large group of Nez Perce against the government when agents attempted to force them onto a reservation.

The Nez Perce fought the army on several occasions and generally outmaneuvered every attempt to recapture them. Finally, in 1877, Chief Joseph and 750 followers, including women and children, made a run for the Canadian border to escape the hands of the army, only to be captured in northern Montana. During the previous four months Chief Joseph and his people had fought 2,000 U.S. troops and 18 Indian auxiliary detachments through two major battles and 18 skirmishes. But, in the end, his people were placed on a reservation in Oklahoma.

By 1880 nearly every Indian tribe in America had been subdued, removed from their traditional lands, and forced onto reservations. As early as 1871 the U.S. government had stopped recognizing the Indians as sovereign nations with legitimate land claims, thus ending the era of treaty making. The new government policy became one of assimilation. This government approach to Indians was embodied in the Dawes Severalty Act, passed by Congress in 1887. Under this act, the reservation lands were broken up and distributed to individual Indians in allotments of 160 acres (65 ha) for each family head. This ended the era of communal ownership of Indian property. Such Indians were encouraged to farm, but few either wanted to or understood how. The days of the once powerful Indian nations of the American West were over.

THE END OF THE FRONTIER

The 1890s signaled a turning point in the history of the American West. The signs were everywhere that the frontier movement was winding down, the hectic days of westward expansion were being tamed, and the lands of the Great Plains and the Far West were not only largely occupied, but were also generally settled. So much of the rough and tumble nature of the frontier had vanished before the end of the nineteenth century. Americans had realized a dream that had preoccupied their ancestors for generations. The frontier had served as the centerpiece of America's early development and expansion across the vast North American continent. For some, the existence of the frontier and its stages of pioneer movements marked the calendar of American history, serving as a pulse regulating the nation's growth and the development of a uniquely American character.

Now, with the approach of the end of the nineteenth century, the nation would continue to change, recreating itself through further growth in the country's urban centers, spurred by the arrival of millions of foreign faces from Europe. At the same time Americans would look beyond their old borders in search of new markets and a new reach for yet more territory.

Chronology

1848 Gold is discovered in California, launching one of
the largest gold rushes in American history
1850 California becomes a state
1858 Gold is discovered in modern-day Colorado (Kansas
Territory) near present-day Denver
1859 Two Irishmen discover gold in Nevada, which leads
to another gold rush

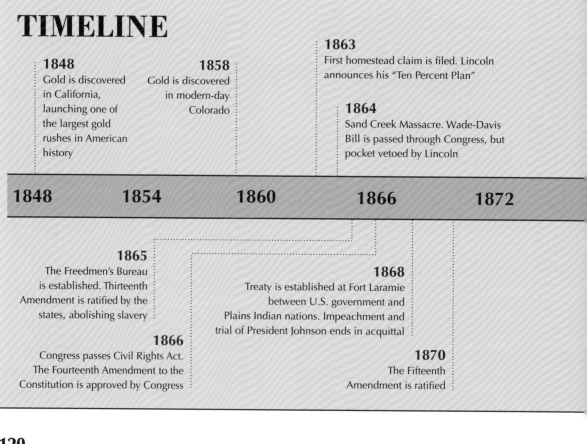

TIMELINE

1848
Gold is discovered in California, launching one of the largest gold rushes in American history

1858
Gold is discovered in modern-day Colorado

1863
First homestead claim is filed. Lincoln announces his "Ten Percent Plan"

1864
Sand Creek Massacre. Wade-Davis Bill is passed through Congress, but pocket vetoed by Lincoln

1848   **1854**   **1860**   **1866**   **1872**

1865
The Freedmen's Bureau is established. Thirteenth Amendment is ratified by the states, abolishing slavery

1866
Congress passes Civil Rights Act. The Fourteenth Amendment to the Constitution is approved by Congress

1868
Treaty is established at Fort Laramie between U.S. government and Plains Indian nations. Impeachment and trial of President Johnson ends in acquittal

1870
The Fifteenth Amendment is ratified

1859–1865 Miners tap $50 million in gold and silver out of the Comstock Lode

1860 The mining community Virginia City, Nevada, is home to 10,000 miners

1862 Gold is discovered along the Boise River Basin in Idaho. Congress passes the Homestead Act, opening up millions of acres of free, western land.

1863 First homestead claim is filed in Beatrice, Nebraska. Lincoln announces his "Proclamation of Amnesty and Reconstruction," which would be known as his "Ten Percent Plan"

1864 Montana Territory is formed. Sand Creek Massacre takes place in eastern Colorado. Wade-Davis Bill is

1874
Gold is discovered in the Dakotas' Black Hills

1883
U.S. Supreme Court declares Civil Rights Act of 1875 to be unconstitutional

1874–1875
Red River War

1886
Apache leader Geronimo surrenders

1873	1878	1884	1890	1896

1875
Congress passes the Civil Rights Act of 1875

1877
Reconstruction ends

1887
Congress enacts the Dawes Severalty Act

1890
Montana, Washington, Wyoming, Idaho, North Dakota, and South Dakota all become states

1876
Custer and the Seventh Cavalry are massacred at the Little Bighorn

passed through Congress, but pocket vetoed by Lincoln

1865 The Freedmen's Bureau is established. Abraham Lincoln is assassinated, and Andrew Johnson becomes president. Mississippi enacts first "black code" legislation. The Ku Klux Klan is created in Tennessee. Thirteenth Amendment is ratified by the states, abolishing slavery. Texas passes the first "separate car law"

1866 Congress passes Civil Rights Act. First of the significant cattle drives out of Texas to destinations in Missouri. That year, two trail men—Charles Goodnight and Oliver Loving—establish the cattle route known as the Goodnight-Loving Trail. The Fourteenth Amendment to the Constitution is approved by Congress

1867 First cattle drives reach the Kansas town of Abilene. Congress passes the First, Second, and Third Reconstruction Acts over President Johnson's veto. Congress also passes the Tenure of Office Act. President Johnson grants amnesty to all Confederates

1868 Treaty is established at Fort Laramie between U.S. government and Plains Indian nations, including Lakota, Cheyenne, Arapaho, and others. Impeachment and trial of President Johnson ends in acquittal. Thaddeus Stevens dies. First black member of the House of Representatives is elected. Ulysses S. Grant is elected president

1870 The Fifteenth Amendment is ratified, giving the vote to all male citizens, regardless of color

1871 U.S. government ends practice of recognizing Indians as sovereign nations with legitimate land claims, which ends the era of treaty making

1872–1874 Non-Indian hunters kill as many as three million bison annually

1873 Discovery of the "Big Bonanza," the largest silver vein found in the Comstock Lode

1874 Gold is discovered in the Dakotas' Black Hills, leading to white intrusion on Indian lands

1874–1875 Red River War fought, with Kiowas, Comanches, and Apaches engaging the U.S. Army

1875 Congress passes the Civil Rights Act of 1875

1876 Colorado becomes a state. Full-scale war breaks out between northern plains native groups and the U.S. Army. Custer and the 7th Cavalry are massacred at the Little Bighorn (Greasy Grass)

1877 Chief Joseph and the Nez Perce are captured in northern Montana after months of fighting with the U.S. Army. Reconstruction ends

1880 The first automatic "combine" is at work in American fields

1883 U.S. Supreme Court declares Civil Rights Act of 1875 to be unconstitutional

1884 Meeting of Western Kansas Cattle Growers' Association calls for end of annual summer cattle drives from Texas

1886 Apache leader Geronimo surrenders

1886–1887 Dry summer and bitter, snowy winter decimates western cattle herds, marking the end of the heyday of the cattle industry in the West

1887 Congress enacts the Dawes Severalty Act

1890 Montana, Washington, Wyoming, Idaho, North Dakota, and South Dakota all become states

Glossary

abolitionism The process of ending slavery.

assimilation The process of gradually adopting, then blending in with, the culture of another, larger group.

black codes Laws passed to limit the personal freedoms of free blacks.

Bleeding Kansas An era of violence in Kansas Territory during the mid to late 1850s, which pitted antislavery supporters and proslavery advocates against one another.

bonanza A mining strike of extraordinary scope and value.

border state One of the slave states that did not secede from the Union and become a Confederate state.

carpetbagger A Northerner who went South following the Civil War to participate in Southern state and local government.

chaps A protective article of clothing, usually leather, worn over pants to protect the wearer's legs.

Confederates or Confederacy Those who supported secession from the United States and who fought for the South during the Civil War.

cow town In the American West, a settlement on the Great Plains to which cowboys drove cattle to be sold to market.

Dawes Severalty Act The 1887 act of Congress that broke up communal Indian lands and replaced them with an allotment of 160 acres (65 ha) of land to the head of each Indian household, thus encouraging private property rights.

Democrat Party The political party formed during the age of Andrew Jackson, which supported the Jackson presidency.

diggings A slang term used by miners or prospectors to refer to the claim sites where prospecting took place.

draw A small land basin, or valley, into or through which water drains.

Emancipation Proclamation An official announcement made by President Abraham Lincoln in the fall of 1862 that "freed" all slaves held in states in rebellion against the United States.

enfranchise To provide someone with access to voting or other rights of citizenship.

exodusters Blacks who left the South following the Civil War and went west to establish homesteads in Kansas and other western territories.

Federal government The national government that holds power by the will of the people. State power is subordinate to federal power.

Fifteenth Amendment An amendment to the Constitution, passed in 1870, which required that no person should be deprived of the vote on the basis of race.

Fourteenth Amendment An amendment to the Constitution, passed by Congress in 1867, which provided former slaves with their full rights of citizenship.

Great American Desert An early nineteenth-century term referring to the Great Plains of North America.

hardrock mining The process of mining deep underground and through solid rock.

Homestead Act An 1862 Congressional act, which promised 160 acres (65 ha) of free western land to any American citizen or foreign immigrant over the age of 21 who was head of a household.

hydraulic mining A form of placer mining that uses a powerful stream of water shooting through a large nozzle to move mineral-bearing gravel.

impeach To charge a serving official with a crime or misdemeanor.

indict To formally accuse someone of a crime or misdemeanor.

Log Cabin Bill An 1841 Act of Congress, which allowed Americans living on the frontier to occupy land without legal title, or before a legal survey.

militia State military forces who are not regular army troops.

pay dirt In prospecting, excavated earth that contains valuable metals, such as gold or silver.

placer mining Surface excavations by prospectors looking for valuable metals, which involve methods of water washing, such as a gold pan, cradle, or long tom.

plantation A large farming estate, often found in the American South during the eighteenth and early nineteenth centuries, where slavery was typically in practice. Plantations often used a large number of slaves.

pocket veto A constitutional option which allows the President to kill a bill by merely refusing to sign it.

prospector An individual searching for gold or other precious metals using simple techniques.

railhead The end of a railroad line; the terminus.

ratification The acceptance of a proposed amendment to the Constitution by two-thirds of the states, making the proposed amendment into law.

Reconstruction The restoration of the South into the United States during the years following the Civil War (1865–1877).

redeemers White southerners who sought to restore their control over southern politics following the Civil War.

Republicans Those holding membership or identity in the Republican Party, which was formed during the early 1850s and was generally a Northern party in its base.

scalawag A name given by white Southerners to leaders and pro-Union whites across the South following the Civil War.

secede To separate or remove a state from a larger state.

State rights The political theory that proposes that the rights of the states come first, over the power of the federal government.

strike A slang term, used by miners or prospectors, for the discovery of precious metals on one's claim site.

suffrage The right to vote.

Ten Percent Plan Lincoln's proposed plan for restoring the Union following the Civil War. The plan allowed a Confederate state to rejoin the United States after a number of people equivalent to 10 percent or more of those voting in the 1860 election had pledged loyalty oaths to the federal government.

Thirteenth Amendment An amendment to the U.S. Constitution, passed in 1865, which brought an official end to slavery in the United States.

Trans-Mississippi West The lands lying west of the Mississippi River, including the Great Plains and the Rocky Mountain region.

unconstitutional Not in accordance with the principles set out in the U.S. Constitution

vaquero A Spanish, or later Mexican, cowboy, the forbearer of the American cowboy of the nineteenth century.

"Waving the blood shirt" A post-Civil War Republican political tactic of reminding voters that Democrats had been the party of secession and rebellion that had divided the country during the Civil War.

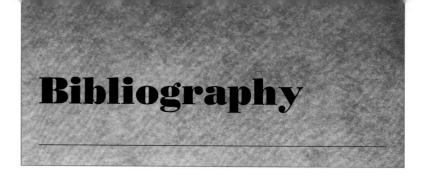

Bibliography

Bartlett, Richard. *The New Country: A Social History of the American Frontier, 1776–1890.* New York: Oxford University Press, 1974.

Brady, Cyrus Townsend. *Indian Fights and Fighters.* Lincoln: University of Nebraska Press, 1971.

Brown, Dee. *Bury My Heart at Wounded Knee: An Indian History of the American West.* New York: Henry Holt and Company, 1970.

Browne, J. Ross. *A Peep at Washoe and Washoe Revisited.* Balboa Island: Paisano Press, 1959.

Dykstra, R. R. "The Cattle Kingdom." *From The West, an Illustrated History.* Henry Steele Commager, ed. New York: Promontory Press, 1976.

Fireside, Harvey. *Separate and Unequal: Homer Plessy and the Supreme Court Decision That Legalized Racism.* New York: Carroll & Graf Publishers, 2004.

Foner, Eric. *Reconstruction: America's Unfinished Revolution, 1863–1877.* New York: Harper & Row. Publishers, 1988.

Forbis, William H. *The Cowboys.* New York: Time-Life Books, 1973.

Hine, Darlene Clark. *The African-American Odyssey.* Upper Saddle River, NJ: Prentice Hall, 2005.

Hine, Robert V. and John Mack Faragher. *Frontiers: A Short History of the American West.* New Haven: Yale University Press, 2007.

Lewis, Jon E. *The Mammoth Book of the West: The Making of the American West.* New York: Carroll & Graf Publishers, 2001.

Milner, Clyde A., Carol A. O'Connor, and Martha A. Sandweiss. *The Oxford History of the American West.* New York: Oxford University Press, 1994.

Roark, James, et al. *The American Promise: A History of the United States*, Volume I. Boston: Bedford / St. Martin's Press, 2009.

Smith, Gene. *High Crimes and Misdemeanors: The impeachment and Trial of Andrew Johnson*. New York: William Morrow and Company, Inc., 1977.

Spence, C. "Riches in the Land." *From The West, an Illustrated History*. Henry Steele Commager, ed. New York: Promontory Press, 1976.

Trefousse, Hans L. *Andrew Johnson: A Biography*. New York: W. W. Norton & Company, 1989.

Utley, Robert and Wilcomb E. Washburn. *Indian Wars*. Boston: Houghton Mifflin Company, 1977.

"Wade-Davis Manifesto." *New York Tribune*, August 5, 1864.

Wallace, Robert. *The Miners*. Alexandria, VA: Time-Life Books, 1976.

Ward, Geoffrey. *The West: An Illustrated History*. Boston: Little, Brown and Company, 1996.

Weinstein, Allen and David Rubel. *The Story of America: Freedom and Crisis From Settlement to Superpower*. New York: DK Publishing, Inc., 2002.

Further Resources

Backus, Harriet. *Tomboy Bride: A Woman's Personal Account of Life in Mining Camps of the West.* Boulder, CO: Pruett Publishing Company, 1980.

Barney, William L. *Civil War and Reconstruction: A Student Companion.* New York: Oxford University Press, 2001.

Behrman, Carol H. *Indian Wars.* Minneapolis: Lerner Publishing Group, 2004.

Boyles, Kate. *The Homesteaders.* Whitefish, MT: Kessinger Publishing Company, 2007.

Conrotto, Eugene L. *Lost Gold and Silver Mines of the Southwest.* Mineola, NY: Dover Publications, 1996.

Freedman, Russell. *In the Days of the Vaqueros: America's First True Cowboys.* New York: Houghton Mifflin, 2001.

Hatt, Christine. *American West.* Mankato, MN: Black Rabbit Books, 2004.

Haugen, Brenda. *Crazy Horse: Sioux Warrior.* Mankato, MN: Coughlan Publishing, 2005.

King, David C. *Civil War and Reconstruction.* Hoboken, NJ: John Wiley & Sons, Inc., 2003.

Matuz, Roger. *Reconstruction Era.* San Diego, CA: Gale Research, Inc., 2004.

Monroe, Judy. *Chief Red Cloud, 1822–1909.* Mankato, MN: Capstone Press, Inc., 2004.

Painter, Nell Irvin. *Exodusters: Black Migration to Kansas After Reconstruction.* New York: Alfred A. Knopf, Inc., 1977.

Price, Sean. *Crooks, Cowboys, and Characters: The Wild West.* Mankato, MN: Raintree Publishers, 2007.

Randolph, Ryan P. *Black Cowboys.* New York: Rosen Publishing Group, 2003.

Stanley, George Edward. *Era of Reconstruction and Expansion, 1865–1900.* Strongsville, OH: Gareth Stevens Publishing, 2005.

Stewart, Elinore Pruitt. *Letters of a Woman Homesteader.* Mineola, NY: Dover Publications, 2006.

Stroud, Bettye. *Reconstruction Era.* Tarrytown, NY: Marshall Cavendish, Inc., 2006.

Uschan, Michael V. *Battle of Little Bighorn.* Chicago: Gareth Stevens Publishing, 2002.

Web sites

Andrew Johnson:
http://www.andrewjohnson.com/
http://www.whitehouse.gov/history/presidents/aj17.html
http://statelibrary.dcr.state.nc.us/nc/bio/public/johnson.htm

Cowboys and outlaws:
http://www.liu.edu/cwis/cwp/library/african/west/west.htm
http://www.thewildwest.org/interface/index.php?action=186
http://www.gunslinger.com/west.html

Exodusters:
http://middle.usm.k12.
wi.us/faculty/taft/unit5/westwebquest/exodusters/

History and legends:
http://www.legendsofamerica.com/LA-OldWestLegends.html
http://www.americanwest.com/index2.htm
http://www.pbs.org/weta/thewest/

Homestead Act:
http://www.archives.gov/education/lessons/homestead-act/

Mining:
http://www.westernmininghistory.com/

Reconstruction:
http://www.digitalhistory.uh.edu/reconstruction/index.html
http://afroamhistory.about.com/od/reconstruction/
    Reconstruction.htm
http://www.pbs.org/wgbh/amex/reconstruction/
http://americanhistory.about.com/od/reconstruction/
    Reconstruction_Era.htm
http://thomaslegion.net/reconstruction.html

Picture Credits

Page

11: The Granger Collection, NYC/TopFoto

20: The Granger Collection, NYC/TopFoto

29: The Granger Collection, NYC/TopFoto

39: The Granger Collection, NYC/TopFoto

43: Illustration by John James

52: The Granger Collection, NYC/TopFoto

61: The Granger Collection, NYC/TopFoto

66: The Granger Collection, NYC/TopFoto

76: The Granger Collection, NYC/TopFoto

81: The Granger Collection, NYC/TopFoto

84: The Granger Collection, NYC/TopFoto

93: The Granger Collection, NYC/TopFoto

99: Illustration by John James

108: The Granger Collection, NYC/TopFoto

110: The Granger Collection, NYC/TopFoto

117: The Granger Collection, NYC/TopFoto

136: Courtesy of Abbott Studio, www.abbottsudio.com

Index

About the Author

Tim McNeese is associate professor of history at York College in York, Nebraska. Professor McNeese holds degrees from York College, Harding University, and Missouri State University. He has published more than 100 books and educational materials. His writing has earned him a citation in the library reference work, *Contemporary Authors* and multiple citations in *Best Books for Young Teen Readers*. In 2006, Tim appeared on the History Channel program, *Risk Takers, History Makers: John Wesley Powell and the Grand Canyon*. He was been a faculty member at the Tony Hillerman Writers Conference in Albuquerque. His wife, Beverly, is assistant professor of English at York College. They have two married children, Noah and Summer, and three grandchildren—Ethan, Adrianna, and Finn William. Tim and Bev have sponsored college study trips on the Lewis and Clark Trail and to the American Southwest. You may contact Professor McNeese at tdmcneese@york.edu.

About the Consultant

Richard Jensen is Research Professor at Montana State University, Billings. He has published 11 books on a wide range of topics in American political, social, military, and economic history, as well as computer methods. After taking a Ph.D. at Yale in 1966, he taught at numerous universities, including Washington, Michigan, Harvard, Illinois-Chicago, West Point, and Moscow State University in Russia.